AMERICAN

★ GUIDE TO PICKING ★

PICKERS

AMERICAN

★ GUIDE TO PICKING ★

PICKERS

LIBBY CALLAWAY WITH **MIKE WOLFE,**
FRANK FRITZ, AND **DANIELLE COLBY**

HYPERION

NEW YORK

Library of Congress Cataloging-in-Publication Data

Callaway, Libby.
  American pickers guide to picking / Libby Callaway with Mike Wolfe, Frank Fritz, and Danielle Colby. — 1st ed.
        p.   cm.
  ISBN 978-1-4013-2448-3
  1. Antiques business—United States.   2. Flea markets—United Sates.
I. American pickers.   II. Title.
  NK1133.28.C35 2011
  745.1075—dc22   2011015146

Hyperion books are available for special promotions and premiums. For details contact the HarperCollins Special Markets Department in the New York office at 212-207-7528, fax 212-207-7222, or e-mail spsales@harpercollins.com.

FIRST EDITION

Book design by Renato Stanisic

10 9 8 7 6 5 4 3 2 1

THIS LABEL APPLIES TO TEXT STOCK

We try to produce the most beautiful books possible, and we are also extremely concerned about the impact of our manufacturing process on the forests of the world and the environment as a whole. Accordingly, we've made sure that all of the paper we use has been certified as coming from forests that are managed, to ensure the protection of the people and wildlife dependent upon them.

Dedicated to the memory of Robert Easterly—my Papaw,
who scored the best pick ever: my Granny, Mildred.

CONT

ENTS

ACKNOWLEDGMENTS

Many thanks to Susan Werbe, Kate Winn, and Robert Brande at HISTORY; Julie Cooper at Cineflix; Elizabeth Sabo and Christine Pride at Hyperion; my attorney, Matt Adams; the marvelously organized Jodi Faeth (Mike is lucky to have you!); and my friends Alexandra Cirimelli, Ruby Guidara, and all the other professionals who provided advice and anecdotes for the book. I'd also like to send sincere appreciation to my family for their love and patience, including my sisters, Millie Callaway and Marie Callaway Kellner; my brother-in-law, Jeff Kellner (thanks for being my guinea pig!); my dad, Mike, a pinch-hit editor extraordinaire; and my mother, Phyllis, who, along with my aunt, Jane Easterly, and our elegant friends Bene Deacon and the late Gaye Romaine, taught me that flea markets were wonderful, magical places. Thanks also to the staff at East Nashville's Ugly Mugs, where I wrote seventy-five percent of this book sitting on their big red couch; and my supportive friends: Bob S. Quinn, Laura Lee Dobie, Pamela Cole, Leigh Maples, Laura and Sam Powers, David McClister and Gina Binkley, Matt and Carrie Eddmenson, and—most of all—the amazing Kristin Barlowe, my creative mentor and the person who introduced me to Mike Wolfe. Thank you all from the bottom of my heart.

AMERICAN

★ GUIDE TO PICKING ★

PICKERS

INTRODUCTION

Just What the Heck Is a Picker, Anyway?

I've never been able to pass a roadside flea market without stopping.

That probably has a lot to do with the conditioning I received as a kid. Much of my childhood was spent traveling to fleas across the South with my mother, an antique dealer who specialized in wicker furniture and sold out of her own store, situated in a repurposed 1920s stone gas station in our hometown of Cleveland, Tennessee.

Mom loved to shop for the Callaway Collection, the name she gave her antique store. It was only open during the week, so, bright and early every Saturday morning, we'd climb into Mom's purple-and-white cargo van (a custom paint job that represented the colors of the CC logo) and head out to one of the regular markets where her favorite vendors—pickers, she called them—set up temporary shop.

On the first weekend, we'd drive north on I-75 to shop the vendors set up on the fairgrounds in Knoxville; the next, we'd take the same interstate south to get to Atlanta's flea; on the third Saturday, we'd head west on I-24 to find out what the pickers in Nashville had picked up over the four weeks since we last saw them.

There was no rest for the wicker-obsessed in our house, so, on the fourth weekend, the Callaway Collection van would take road trips into the nearby Appalachian Mountains to seek out obscure antique stores or drop in on some of my mom's favorite contacts. I recognized the men and women we'd visit from the flea markets, where they'd set up booths, but my mom liked to also visit them at their homes or workshops, where she could see their whole collections and not just what they were able to fit into their booths at the market.

Sometimes, if a picker had just come off a big buying trip where they scored lots of wicker—my mother explained to me that she didn't have time to find all the stock she needed to fill her store, so the pickers were helping her do it—they would come directly to our house. It was a favor to my mom, as one of their loyal customers: they'd let her see their best picks first.

I have vivid memories of those visits. I can recall being up very early on some summer mornings when I was three or four, driving my Big Wheel in big circles around the end of our driveway, which was, at the time, blocked by a flatbed truck loaded up with a massive jumble of furniture, each piece connected to the next by a tenuous-looking web of twine and cording. You know the intro to *The Beverly Hillbillies* TV show, where the Clampett family pulls into Los Angeles with all their belongings tied to the top of their creaky old jalopy—including Granny Clampett, sitting atop the pile in her rocking chair? Our truck looked like that, minus Granny.

I specifically remember visits from a flatbed manned by two stout, serious-looking dudes with unruly facial hair and suntanned, wind-chapped faces and hands. They were men of few words, and would stand by their truck, at the ready, waiting patiently for my mom to point at pieces of wicker trapped in their latticework of secondhand furniture, which she wanted to examine up close. Once she made her selection, the two men would climb up on the pile, untie the piece, and bring it down to the ground for Mom to inspect. After checking out the construction, looking for obvious flaws, and weighing whether it would appeal to her clientele and their proto–Shabby Chic style, Mom would make her decision.

If she wanted to buy, the negotiation process would begin. She'd ask the pickers for a price; they'd give her a number and she'd think for a minute and she'd come back at them with a lower counteroffer . . . that they'd quickly raise with their own counter-offer. This kind of back-and-forth went on until both Mom and the pickers came to a price that made both parties happy.

If Mom decided to pass on the piece, our sweaty visitors would hoist the wicker love seat or end table or birdcage or whatever it was they were hawking that day (their stock was always different) back up to a place atop the pile and tie it in tight for the trip to the home of their next client.

MORE THAN THIRTY years later, as I think back on those visits, I realize that my child's perspective was surely a bit skewed.

The reality is that, more than likely, the guys I recall as being rough around the edges probably weren't all that grungy. And I'm guessing they weren't very old, either—they must have been in their forties, about the age I am now. (Their truck, however, definitely looked like a prop from *The Beverly Hillbillies*—that I'm pretty clear on.)

I think it was because of my early experiences with pickers that I was so surprised when I met Mike Wolfe for the first time. I couldn't believe this guy was a picker: young, handsome, and charming, his whole persona seemed antithetical to that of the quiet, subdued pickers who worked with my mom back in the 70s.

Mike and I met on a photo shoot held on a freezing Sunday in early December of 2008, at a prop house located in a little town called Watertown, just a few miles outside Nashville, where I live. I was the wardrobe stylist for the project; Mike had stopped by to visit the photographer, our mutual friend, whom he and his picking partner, Frank Fritz, had met several years before, when the two of them used to drive down from their home base in eastern Iowa to set up together at the Nashville flea market.

That day, when Mike told me what he did, I was intrigued, and I instantly felt the kind of easy rapport with him that people who share a passion tend to develop. My initial fascination with my new picker friend quickly changed to admiration a few hours later, when I saw him in action for the first time.

It was a long, cold shoot, and even the fact that we were photographing two gorgeous girls dressed up in 1930s bondage wear and lingerie couldn't hold Mike's interest for more than a few minutes. He was getting bored—like that of 99 percent of the picker population, his attention span can be measured in seconds as opposed to minutes—so he asked to borrow a scooter from Ruby, the prop house's owner (you'll meet her later in the book), to take a ride around the tiny town and check it out. "I'll be back!" Mike said, as he pulled away.

And, in less than thirty minutes, he *was* back—with a pristine, green, two-sided, enamel Oliver Tractor sign from the 40s under his arm and a huge grin on his face.

Ruby was blown away. "I thought I'd seen every cool antique in this town. Where the heck did you find that?" she asked. Mike explained that while he was out tooling around, he spotted a house that, in his words, "looked promising"—which, I quickly came to realize, means slightly rundown and surrounded by crabgrass as opposed to well-kept and manicured.

Why don't I just let him explain what happened:

Whenever I go to a new place, I try to get my bearings and figure out what the town is all about. I'm always curious. The reason I stopped at that place that day was because the guy had this really old building behind his house that looked like a service station. It was really large and had big doors, and seemed to have lots inside: from the street, I could tell that there were things piled up in front of the windows, which is a good sign to a picker.

So, I pulled the bike over and knocked on the door. An older gentleman answered, and I introduced myself. I told him I was from Iowa, that I was a picker—and I had to explain what a picker is. I have to do that a lot, actually: not many people know what a picker does, or they think I play banjo or something—and that I was looking for old bikes, cars, signs, and other collectible items that he might want to let go of.

I asked him about the building behind the house. I was right; it was a garage, and had been in his family for a long time. He started going into a lot of detail, saying that it was his dad's and then he ran it. I love to hear that kind of thing: I love the backstory and let people tell me what they're passionate about. To this guy, it was his property, and I let him tell me about it—I wanted to hear it. After we talked for a while, he loosened up and started to trust me. Then he was happy to show me the stone garage.

One of the first things I saw was the Oliver sign. It was two-sided, which makes it more valuable than signs that are only printed on one side, and it was in great shape. We both agreed it was a nice piece.

I told him I'd give him $35 for it.

"No, I can't do that."

Then would you take $60?

He hesitated for a minute; I could tell that he knew it was a good deal, but that something was keeping him from selling. So, I asked him what he was planning on doing with the sign. "Well, I'm probably not going to do anything with it." I told him that in that case, I'd give him $65 to get it off his hands

and take it out of the straw in his barn and back into the
public, where someone else could enjoy it. He liked that idea;
it got through to him.
    Sold.

The story only gets better. Not two minutes after Mike rolled back into the warehouse, he sold it to Ruby for $150.

Sold—again!

In less than an hour, Mike had more than doubled his money, had a mini-adventure in a new town, and made a new friend while doing it—in other words, it was a typical day in Pickerville.

I'm pretty sure my jaw was on the floor the whole time I was watching this scene unfold back at the prop house. Hearing about Mike's door-knocking approach was totally new to me. As I said, I'd been around pickers many times before, but until Mike came into my life, I'm not sure I ever really appreciated the skill associated with what they did.

One thing that I am sure of: I've never met two men who take as much pride in their work as Mike and Frank do.

THANKS TO MY mom's influence, I grew up loving antiques and embracing the thrill of the hunt. And even though I've had all sorts of collections over the years—crazy quilts, Deco powder compacts, lacquered Chinese boxes, portraits of women (my "lady painting" collection is eighty pieces strong)—I have become somewhat of a vintage clothing hound, in large part due to the knowledge I've gained and shopping opportunities I've been afforded through my job as a fashion journalist.

I spent most of my twenties in New York City, where I became a regular on the thrift store and consignment store circuit and faithfully made weekend-morning pilgrimages to the now closed 26th Street Flea Market in Chelsea. There, among long tables covered in dusty antique jewelry and bins filled with vintage styles from every decade imaginable, I was in heaven. Church held little appeal for me back then; the flea was my Sunday-morning ritual.

I don't discriminate: I'll shop wherever I can find quality junk, from consignment stores and antique malls to estate sales and swap meets. Above all, I prefer thrift shops. I think their appeal lies in the strong concentration of clothes available at thrifts, something you don't always get if you're at an antique mall. Also, thrift shops are plentiful: not every city has a flea market, but practically every town I've ever visited has at least one Goodwill or St. Vincent de Paul or a branch of one of the other big thrift chains, some of which span the globe (I should know: I've thrifted on four continents and counting).

Needless to say, I consider myself a pretty hard-core secondhand shopper. I'm ruthless when it comes to getting the best deal I can, and can negotiate with the best of them. I don't mind getting dirty or shopping in grungy neighborhoods if the outcome will lead to killer finds.

But door-knocking? No, thank you. As truly exciting as Mike's and Frank's signature method sounds—and as many times as I've been tempted to stop at an awesomely junked-up house I come across on a drive, and ask for a grand tour—I'm too reserved to march right up to a stranger's door as they do.

And that's why Mike and Frank are the ones doling out the advice and giving up the anecdotes in this book based on their hit TV series, *American Pickers*. I'm just their conduit—the "picker whisperer," if you will. Using my unique perspective as both a professional journalist and a semi-pro picker, I've selected the best advice and most fascinating stories from the series and combined them with some of Mike's and Frank's personal tips and tales, with some conventional wisdom thrown in for good measure.

In the book, Mike and Frank discuss the logistics of their job, including finding good places to pick (the details that make a property a "good pick" will surprise you!), the importance of making a connection and keeping in touch with potential sellers; the negotiation process; how to market and sell your picks; and, finally, how pickers can expect their jobs to change in the future. The book also includes guidance from Danielle Colby, the pickers' dedicated Girl Friday, as well as thoughts on collecting and selling from some of the guys' favorite go-to experts in the antiques and design industries and other creative fields.

This book is written in what's called a collective voice. Unless it's indicated in the text—when Mike, Frank, Danielle, or one of the experts we spoke to has something especially smashing to say, their idea is introduced and then printed in italics, like Mike's story about Watertown was earlier in this chapter—none of the words here can be directly attributed to one specific person. The voice isn't Mike's or Frank's, nor is it mine; it's ours, together.

One thing to remember as you're reading this book: you don't have to knock on strangers' doors to qualify as a picker. Mike's and Frank's upfront method might not be your bag; that's okay. As I explained, I pretty much limit my picking to thrift stores and flea markets, yet I identify myself as a picker through and through. You can say the same thing whether you're most comfortable shopping at estate sales, antique malls, consignment stores, auctions, or even on the Internet. Your means may be different than Mike's and Frank's, but goal is the same: scoring amazing secondhand treasures.

That's enough from me. Without further ado, let's bring in Mike Wolfe and Frank Fritz, the American Pickers themselves:

A PICKER'S LIFE FOR US

What does a picker do? We get that question all the time.

Pickers are kind of a cross between Indiana Jones and Sanford & Son. Basically, we're professional treasure hunters, but instead of precious artifacts, we're on the lookout for good old all-American junk—aka rusty gold.

Most pickers don't deal in fine antiques; we leave that up to the antique dealers, some of whom are our clients. Pickers are on the lookout for those of the down-and-dirty—and sometimes even bizarre—variety: old bicycles and vintage tools, sun-bleached cars and handmade furniture, retired carnival games and weird taxidermy are always on their shopping list.

We're both based out of Le Claire, Iowa, but you'll rarely find us there. Pickers travel—a lot. You don't uncover the one-of-a-kind things we're in the market for by staying in one place for very long. We're always burning up the back roads, taking the routes less traveled, keeping our eyes open for properties that look like they might be holding hidden jewels.

Once we find a good-looking spot—and "good-looking" to us

YARD TALK

What to look for and what to avoid when you're looking for pickable properties:

GOOD:	BAD:
Older neighborhoods	McMansions
Un-renovated houses	Satellite dishes
Single-family homes	Aboveground pools
Outbuildings: sheds, barns, garages	Kid toys in the driveway
"Vintage" paint colors: pink, avocado, harvest gold	Manicured yards and landscaping
Cars parked in the front yard	Fresh paint-jobs and new roofing
Un-mowed lawns and tall weeds	Modern architecture
Rust—on anything, anywhere	Shiny new cars and lawn mowers
Old tractors	Swing sets

means things like overgrown bushes and unmowed yards; sagging roofs or ones covered by tarps; lots of random outbuildings, preferably aged and unpainted; rusty farm equipment scattered across the front yard; and cars parked in the front yard—we walk right up to the front door, give it a knock, and then ask whomever answers if we can look around. If they agree to let us go through their barn or garage or attic or shed or pig pen or wherever else they've stashed their junk, we're ready to rock.

Haggling is the name of the game in picking. If we find something we like, we try to get the best deal we can. Most of the things we buy we plan to resell, either to one of the hundreds of private clients we have all around the world (in the mix are dealers, collectors, design pros, and artsy people like photographers and art directors, who tend to dig our funkier stuff) or at Antique Archaeology, the business Mike owns back in Le Claire.

Except for rare occasions when we want to go in together to buy a big item that we can't afford on our own, each of us buys and sells our finds separately. Even though Frank is considered a member of the Antique Archaeology team, he doesn't work for Mike. The two of us aren't business partners; we're picking partners. And yes, there's a difference.

We're able to pick together because, in most cases, we buy different things. Frank likes antique metal toys, petroleum collectibles, vending machines, and other interesting mechanical contraptions. Mike is a bit more eclectic in his tastes, and has a real appreciation for far-out items like weird taxidermy and folk art, as well as an enduring love for bicycles of all kinds.

We do have one big crossover area: we both collect items that have to do with transportation—specifically, motorcycles. But even when we're talking motorcycles, our interests are different enough that we rarely compete: Mike likes pre-1920s American bikes and parts, while Frank is into comparatively newer dirt bikes and choppers and Japanese brands like Kawasaki, Honda, and Yamaha.

When we come across something we both like—say, a mint-condition porcelain sign advertising a 1940s gas station that has big, colorful graphics and a cool catch phrase (like Exxon's "Put a Tiger in Your Tank")—we try to be diplomatic about it. The guy who discovered it gets first dibs; if he decides to pass, the other man can move in and make a bid. This actually happens much less frequently than you'd think it would. Most of the places we pick are very large and packed with so much stuff that it's pretty self-defeating to get too preoccupied with one item out of thousands. Picking is like any other fast-paced business: time is money.

Our secret to making a profit is that we skip the middleman, meaning we don't buy from thrift stores, antique malls, or flea markets. Instead, we go straight to the source. This involves a ton of time on the road (we put sixty thousand miles on our van every year) and even more time spent preparing. Good pickers do a lot of homework—you have to, if you want to stay on top of the game.

Since we're on the road so much, we depend on Antique Archaeology's business manager, Danielle, to do most of this for us. She stays back at Antique Archaeology, and spends her days (as well as a lot of her nights: picking is a 24/7 affair) scanning Craigslist and antique industry blogs for ideas; comparing prices of things we want to sell with the final bids of auctions on eBay; putting "wanted to buy" ads in the classified sections of collectors' magazines and newspapers in cities we plan to visit; and cold-calling small-town Chamber of Commerce offices and little regional museums, asking for leads. Any lead is a good one if it takes us to awesome stuff.

BALLAD OF MIKE AND FRANK

Neither of us has any formal training in the history of antiques. Everything we've learned about collectibles during all the years we've been picking for a living has come from on-the-job experience and quizzing the huge team of expert appraisers and dealers that we've met on the job for help.

But the good thing about picking as a duo is that we can play expert to each other. We've known each other since we were in junior high school back in Iowa, so there's a lot of trust there.

We both started picking when we were little kids. When Frank was growing up in Davenport, he started looking for coins, stamps, interesting rocks—typical kids' collections. He liked beer cans, too:

I started picking by accident. There were some railroad tracks in the woods between my house and my elementary school, which I wasn't supposed to walk through; my mom wanted me to stay on the sidewalks. I didn't listen. Railroad tracks ran through the woods, and hobos used to set up camps there, places for them to rest when they weren't riding a rail, and they'd leave things behind. Sometimes they'd still be there, drinking, and get up and chase us off. But they never caught up; they were kind of slow and we were young kids. We could run fast.

We'd go back when they finally left their camp and find lots of beer cans—the old-fashioned cone-topped ones. I used to pick them up and bring them home. Collecting those was fun, because you could challenge yourself to collect different brands and look for different graphics.

Mike did the beer-can thing, too; poking around the woods behind his house, abandoned alleys, and junkyards he'd play in after school. But his big interest has always been bicycles. In his twenties, before he went pro as a picker, Mike raced bikes competitively and owned a bike shop in Davenport. But he was already selling them well before that: Mike was only six when he flipped his first bike, the best of a bunch that he pulled out of his neighbor's Tuesday-morning garbage pile on his way to school.

I couldn't believe that they'd throw these things away—they were so beautiful to me, even all piled up in the trash. Most were current models—meaning, from the 60s—and had those long banana seats. They were in pretty good shape, too.

I took them all home and kept them in the garage, which my mom had given me to hold my collections. Until then, I didn't have a bike of my own. So I chose the one from the pile that I liked the most, cleaned it up, and put air in the tires. Then I rode it down the street to where all the older kids were hanging out. One of them saw it and said, "Hey! I'll give you five dollars for that bike." I was like, okay! Back in '69, that was a lot of money, man! Five dollars was a huge deal to a little kid.

So, from then on, I kept my eyes open. I found so much awesome stuff in the garbage: busted-up toy car and monster model kits, books, stickers—things that other kids had thrown away. It blew my mind that they were getting rid of this stuff when I knew it was worth some money. Basically, what other people saw as junk, I saw as opportunity.

Neither of us had any idea of the real value of the stuff we were trading. When you're a kid, you don't think about things being collectible or being antique. You just want to find something that looks cool or that the other kids wanted more than the thing they had.

In junior high and high school, the two of us made the step up from picking and flipping to trading. The idea was to get your hands on something good enough to convince the guy who had the thing you wanted to trade his for yours. The goal was to keep trading up for something better and better each time, until you got to the point where what you had was big enough to cash in for something really good.

For example, let's say Frank found a cassette tape by the band Boston in the garbage (don't judge: this was the 70s). He'd ask around, find out what other people who were into swapping had and what they were looking to buy until he found a Boston fan who needed that album and was willing to trade a pair of his Nike sneakers to get it.

From there, maybe Frank's sneakers would get traded up for a bike seat, which he then would swap for a pair of stereo speakers. The key is supply and demand: find someone who needs what you have and who has something you want, and make a deal. Sometimes you'd end up actually selling the thing you were trying to swap; no problem: money is always a good trade.

We both got really good at trading and ended up with some pretty nice gear: Mike was riding a Miata road bike before he graduated from high school; Frank made enough money swapping and selling to buy a Harley.

Even though we were swapping in the same crowds, the two of us really didn't start hanging out until after high school, when we started running into each other. Mike was running his bike shop, and Frank was working around town as a fire inspector but we were both picking on the side. About fifteen years ago, we started turning up at the same sales and swap meets. We liked a lot of the same things—motorcycle stuff, especially—so the two of us started picking together in our area.

Picking isn't very much fun by yourself. Yes, there is less competition if you go it alone, but it's not as much fun as having a buddy with you on long trips to keep you company. Plus, it's nice to have another set of eyes. We always ask each other, "Hey, how much do you think I should do on this?" "Aw, man, that's junk. But look at this!" Two heads are better than one, so to speak.

About a decade ago, we took our show on the road, hauling things we found here in the Midwest to sell to dealers and at flea markets in other parts of the country. By then, we'd both quit our day jobs and had gone to work for ourselves, as full-time pickers. The rest is history.

Or should we say HISTORY? In 2010, HISTORY channel started airing *American Pickers*, the all-about-picking TV series that follows us across the country as we rescue lost treasures and meet some of the country's most fascinating people. In the lead-in to every episode, Mike's voice-over says, "We make a living telling the history of America, one piece at a time." That's 100 percent true. Just as every person in this great nation has a story all their own, everything we buy on the road has a history all *its* own—and the truly amazing thing is that it doesn't have to be something of major monetary value or huge importance to make an impact on us.

Little objects can speak volumes. Take the hammered-silver-and-turquoise belt buckle inscribed with the words "Carnie Power" that belonged to Bear, a proud retired carnival worker—one of our earliest picks on the series. The buckle had larger historical significance because it also featured an etching of the first-ever Ferris Wheel that debuted at the Chicago World's Fair in 1893; but the personal heft it held for Bear was even greater. He came from a long line of proud carnival employees, and of all the things he owned—and from the looks of his farm, we're talking everything from old signs to bumper cars and everything in between—it was the thing that made him the proudest.

It's coming across those seemingly unimportant things on the job that makes our work so interesting. Yes, it's beyond cool to get a lead on something unusual and valuable when we're out in the field, but truly it's not the big-ticket items like a pre-1920s Excelsior motorcycle that stick with us: it's the people.

We love the things we pick and we respect the people who sell them to us—they're the best part of our job. And this is what separates us from other pickers out there. If someone shows us a piece that they're really excited about, we get excited. We love sharing that moment with them. We love to share their passion.

"HOW CAN I DO WHAT YOU DO?"

We have a motto on the road: Pickin', diggin', junkin', livin'. To us, being out on the road, finding new people to pick, and rescuing cool old stuff from obscurity is definitely good living.

Apparently, a lot of other people out there think the picker's life is the one for them, too. When we're traveling across the United States, filming *American Pickers*, we meet dozens of fans every day, and almost all of them ask us how to get started. Maybe they want to do a little picking on the weekends—dig up some cool stuff and sell it at the flea market to make a little extra dough. Maybe they want to turn their hobby into a career, like we have. This book will tell them how.

If you combine the time that the two of us have each spent in the junk trenches, it adds up to over fifty years. That's half a century of picks. In that time, we've accumulated quite a bit of knowledge when it comes to finding the best places to pick.

We know the things to look for when you're on your search, and have some pretty solid ideas about what you need to avoid. We know the best way to approach a seller—what to say, what not to say, and even when to run. We have tips for how to conduct a search, price your finds, and make a solid deal. Somewhere along the way, we even made up our own lingo, which is in here, too.

This book was written to help aspiring pickers make their adventures easier, safer, and a lot more fun. Keep it with you in the car when you're out on a pick, for quick reference. Or read it aloud to your family at night: kids love picking—a good thing, since they're the future of our business. We're putting all we got out there for your own personal picking; take what you like and leave the rest.

And welcome to the wild world of picking!

Mike Wolfe & Frank Fritz

1
FREE-STYLING

HOW AND WHERE TO FIND GREAT PLACES TO PICK

YOU HAVE TO BE A CHAMELEON IN THIS PROFESSION; YOU HAVE TO ALWAYS BE WILLING TO CHANGE AND BLEND INTO YOUR SURROUNDINGS. AND YOU HAVE TO BE WILLING TO GET DIRTY. AM I ABOVE DUMPSTER DIVING? NO WAY. IF THE SITUATION CALLS FOR IT, I'LL DIVE IN HEADFIRST.

—Mike Wolfe

Pickers have some pretty definite habitats, and they're usually not very pretty. Got dirt? Bring it on, baby. We're not scared of a few stains.

If you watch *American Pickers*, you know the kind of places we're talking about: rough-and-tumble joints like old rundown barns; weed- and rust-covered sheds; lean-tos jutting out of rotting buildings; damp, smelly basements; musty, dark garages only a pigeon could love; dusty abandoned storefronts . . . You get the picture.

When we knock on a door, 90 percent of the time the things we find are junk. But we don't care about the odds; a picker never turns down an opportunity, no matter where it is. We've picked pickup trucks. We've picked flatbeds. We've picked Dumpsters. We even picked a Mercury Sable. We're looking for the unusual, the impossible, the funky, the different, the bizarre—things we have never seen before. And we'll go anywhere we have to go to find it.

No location is off-limits to a hard-core picker. And there's plenty of things to be found at antique stores, thrift and consignment shops, flea markets, estate sales, and swap meets, and a lot of the tips in this book apply to finding treasures at these joints. But that's not really the kind of picking we do anymore. We look outside the box to find our junk—a word we use almost like a term of endearment: to us, junk is beautiful.

In our style of picking, we don't go through a middleman. We don't get our stock from the woman with a booth in the antique mall or the guy who makes his living reselling stuff on eBay. We get ours straight from the source; we deal one-on-one with the owner and buy directly out of his house, garage, barn, warehouse—wherever he stores his collection, that's where we want to be.

WE'RE ON THE road all the time. How much? Let's put it this way: we put tens of thousands of miles on the Antique Archaeology van every year, driving from sea to shining sea in search of remarkable things.

We like to be flexible when we're out of town; it's important for us to be able to feel as though we can turn off onto random dirt roads that catch our eye and see what lies at the end of them. But we never head out without some sort of a plan. We're fine driving out to iffy picks if they're close to home, but we don't drive more than a few hundred miles without having at least three solid leads. Otherwise, we'd be wasting gas, not to mention time.

A lot of our leads come from spending hours on the phone and scouring the Internet. But our favorite way to find picks is to drive into the countryside to see what we can find. It's our idea of freedom—no destination, no deadline, lots of road, an endless supply of opportunities. It's our signature move and we call it free-styling.

When we're free-styling, we always take the road less traveled: back roads in the country and alleys in the city are our favorite routes.

FINDER'S FEES

To folks who give us good leads that pay off, we offer a fee for helping us out. Or, instead of paying them flat-out, maybe we'll give them a discount on a purchase or a good deal on a trade. Or perhaps we'll share the wealth and turn them on to something great, too.

PICKING 101

We keep our eyes wide-open, and drive around looking out the window until we find a property that fits our picking criteria. Then we stop, knock on the owner's door, and ask if we can look around.

So, if we get on a property, give it a good once-over, and decide it seems like it's all quantity and no quality, we're outta there. Chances are another picker has been there already—a major occupational hazard in our line of work. We want to pick first.

Of course, we didn't invent the wheel here with free-styling: junkers have been driving around, knocking on doors since time began. But during our years in the business, we have developed some time-tested moves that can help anyone who wants to give picking a shot.

THE BEAUTY OF free-styling is that you can do it anywhere. There's good stuff in every town, city, and state. But there are certain parts of the country that we think are better than others for the kind of picking we do.

The East Coast is a picker's Mecca; it's where all our picking forefathers have junked before us. You're really walking on sacred picking ground in New England and the mid-Atlantic states, and we get up there whenever we can to bask in the history. Because this is one of the oldest settled parts of the country, the properties there are more likely to have larger and older accumulations. If there was

REGIONAL PICKING

Picking is a regional thing. The stuff that people collect in Montana probably isn't going to be the same as what folks are looking for in Miami. Whether you're picking or selling, it helps to know the market you're headed to before you get there. A good resource is Craigslist, where you can search for specifics under the "For Sale" heading.

PICKING 101

a house on Plymouth Rock that had stuff in the front yard, you can be sure we'd have knocked on the door by now.

You still have to be choosy about where you pick there, though: just because it's where the early colonists came doesn't mean you're going to find a mega-score full of pieces from the *Mayflower* at every stop. A lot of pickers we know like to go to upstate New York, where there are big farmhouses and barns that have been around forever and are still full of older furniture and folk art. No matter how good the finds may be, for the way we like to work it's almost too rural there. There are too many mountains that made it hard for people to build, so you don't find houses at regular intervals. And the towns are spaced pretty far apart, too.

Pennsylvania is better suited to our particular needs. It has a much better mix of urban and rural life. Big farms and small towns— the magic combination for pickers like us, who bank on digging up a wide variety of items as quickly as possible. You can be in, say, the little iron town of Pottstown, doing some alley driving, checking to see if any of the little local businesses have thrown away anything cool—when you're picking urban areas, it's always worth looking by the back door of little businesses to see if they've had a major housecleaning and tossed out some collectible displays or signage, which collectors love to buy—and then be out in the country, scanning the horizon for junked-up farmhouses on a dirt road two minutes later. And then there'll be another town three miles down the road. Boom boom boom. Real fast, high-speed picking. And the quality of the things we find there is amazing; because it was one of the first areas in the United States to be settled, the Atlantic states have the highest concentration of fine furniture and antiques.

The South is tougher. We find it's good for scoring really wacky, weird things, like folk art. You can find some older European pieces from the English settlers and folks moving down from the Mid-Atlantic, and there were also some French antiques that came in via seaports like New Orleans. But a lot of the older things that did come to the South have rotted away in the heat and humidity, which isn't kind to preservation.

The big drawback of picking in the extreme north or the extreme south is the weather. You always have to consider how cold or how hot it's going to be at the time of year you want to pick. Think about it: you don't want to head up to Minneapolis in winter and—believe us—it's not a good time to be in New Orleans when it's 110 degrees outside. The bottom line is that warm, dry weather is best for picking. Spring and fall—transitional seasons—are ideal.

When the weather is nice, you're more likely to run into folks in their yards, which makes approaching them a lot easier than knocking on their door. And you can't underestimate how much the weather influences someone's mood. We want happy sellers at the door, not grouchy ones who are dealing with a whacked-out HVAC. You know, who wants to show off their collections when they've got frozen pipes to deal with?

When we go south of the Mason-Dixon Line, we run into lots of raw, untapped picking areas. To us, coming from the fields of Iowa, where we're based, the setups we see down there are like another planet. Properties go on forever—everything just sprawls. People set up impromptu roadside flea markets on the weekend. Plus, everybody's got all their stuff out in the front yard, which makes our job that much easier.

The Midwest, where we live, is full of picks, too. When settlers were heading out West, sometimes they only made it as far as the Mississippi—big rivers are hard to cross if you're hauling your family and all your worldly possessions. So they stopped and made permanent camps here.

Another reason picking is so rich in our neck of the woods is all the factories that opened here over the last hundred years. Not only were they producing things that people wanted to buy—anything from furniture to cars—they were also bringing workers to the area, workers that bought the furniture and cars that they were pumping out. When these people were done using their stuff, they'd put it in their barn or shed and forget about it. Now, fifty or a hundred years later, here we come, ready to take it off their hands.

WHEN WE FIRST started picking back in the late 80s and early 90s, there was no Internet. You had to network to find picks, meet other collectors and learn how they operated.

Back then, if we were unfamiliar with a town, we'd look for an antique store and ask folks there to help with leads. We'd also drive from town to town, tacking up fliers that listed what we wanted to buy up on the bulletin boards at Laundromats, grocery stores, post offices—anywhere we knew people congregated. We even made it easy on them, and made the fliers with those little rip-off tags at the bottom so people could take the number with them without taking down the sign.

We would run ads in the local newspapers in two or three little towns on the route we planned to drive, as well as those Penny Saver–type magazines you can pick up for free at gas stations. We'd wait until we had enough solid leads, and then head out for a week or two. But, to be honest, the response was never overwhelming; we had enough bites to keep us busy and could make a living, but we had to work a lot harder for a lot less than we do now that we have the World Wide Web at our disposal.

The Internet has changed picking, no doubt about that. People are a lot more likely to check out Craigslist for "wanted" ads than they are to pick up a free paper, so online has become a great source for us. Picking is an old art and we could still do it without our smart phones and laptops. But it sure would take longer.

The great thing about having a cell phone with Internet access on a pick is the immediacy with which we can get things done. If you forget an address, you can look it up again online—heck, you can just plug it into MapQuest, let the computer read your coordinates, and command it to take you there. The time we save not having to worry about using a paper map or depending on a bunch of little slips of paper with names and addresses scrawled across them trashing up the floor of the van is incalculable.

Still, we try to keep in mind that there are plenty of folks out there who don't even have a cell phone—some of them still have dial phones, if you can believe it—let alone a smart phone or a computer that they can use to upload digital pictures of what they're selling. That kind of guy can be either your best friend or your worst enemy.

Here's why. On the phone, the dude tells you that he has amazing stuff that he's never shown to anyone. He's convincing—so much so that he convinces you it's worth driving three hundred miles in the rain to see what he's got. So, you get in your truck, drive to his farm in the middle of nowhere, and all he's got is a bunch of tin cans. What can you do? Sure, you're upset. But what if he was right and his stuff was totally killer? You'd never have known if you hadn't tried.

The truth is that people usually have no idea what they have. We've seen ads where the seller claims she has a garage full of Danish mid-century modern furniture, only to get there and find it's all reproductions—or, as we like to call copies of antiques, repop. Or someone might send you an e-mail promising they have a trunk in their attic that has been in their family for over one hundred years,

STAYING ORGANIZED

Each of us has a different way of keeping up with our contacts. We each keep a stocked cell phone on us at all times (it's essential to back this puppy up on our hard drives on a regular basis), a vast list of e-mails on our computers, and written backups as well in piles of notebooks and folders filled with business cards. Active picks—people and things we are hotly pursuing—are written on the big chalkboard that Danielle keeps up with back at home.

PICKING 101

MID-CENTURY DANISH MODERN FURNITURE

Danish designers had limited resources during WWII and, therefore, worked almost exclusively with natural materials like wood, linen, and clay. These materials are now synonymous with the clean, simple lines of the Danish Modern movement that peaked in the late 50s and early 60s. One of the best-known Danish Modern designers was Finn Juhl, who initially popularized the design and introduced it to America.

which they want to sell. And then you drive a few hundred miles only to find that it was made in the 60s.

Again, it's usually not the seller's fault. We don't run into a lot of people who intentionally mislead us. Many folks just don't know enough about what they're trying to sell to describe it correctly. A lot of the time, the "antique" they're talking about was given to them by someone in their family who told them it was old and valuable when it's really just repop. They're not to blame: they're just passing along information they were given that just happens to be bad. That happens a lot with "family heirlooms."

GETTING A VISUAL of what the seller has to offer is hands-down the best way to go. Like they say, a picture is worth a thousand words.

Pictures can be revealing to pickers in more ways than one. There have been times when we've asked an out-of-town seller to send us a snapshot of a car or bike that we're interested in and been more turned on by the stuff in the background of the shot. It's, like, "The old Ford Fairlane in the picture? Yeah—it's fine. But hey—tell me more about those old gas station signs hanging on the garage wall behind it? Are those for sale?"

But this usually only happens when you're dealing with computer-savvy sellers. Again, the guy who still watches three channels on a black-and-white TV with rabbit ears probably doesn't know any-thing about sending you a digital image. In those cases, you just have to ask a ton of really good questions.

The exact questions we ask when we're talking to a prospective pick change person-to-person. If we're trying to get a feeling for what someone has, we're really general—we ask whether they collect glass or pottery, furniture or tools, bikes or cars. Once we find out what they're into, then we ask about specifics, like what brand of pottery or what style of furniture.

When they bring up an item we're interested in, there are a few things we want to know about it no matter what: the age of the item; how long the seller has had it; where they got it; if it has markings; and what it's made of. Those are the basics. Then we ask every other question that pops into our minds. Sometimes we're on the phone for hours. We ask all these questions because we don't want to drive a thousand miles to pick a place that's already been plucked dry by Jersey John or One-Eyed Paul or one of the thousands of other pickers across the country that we compete with every day. Heck, we don't want to drive ten miles for that.

Even after all this prep, we sometimes still end up on a wild goose chase. And that's when we find ourselves ten hours away from home, in the middle of Nowheresville, South Dakota, sitting in the van with no place to go. And instead of being pissed off or heading back home, we just have to make it happen.

FREE-STYLING IS ALL about being selective. You can't just start knocking on the door of every slightly junked-up house you come across, asking to look inside. There's a method to a picker's madness.

Pickers have a different sense of their surroundings than other people. Even when we're out just driving around the little town of Le Claire, Iowa—the home of Antique Archaeology, our picking HQ—we're always looking out the window, trying to see if anything has changed around us. We look between houses and check out what's been left in the spaces behind garages and buildings. Stuff tends to get dumped there, sometimes overnight. You never know when or where cool things will turn up, so we're always looking.

When we hit a new town in search of new picks, we don't head to the rich parts of town. We look for older middle- and working-class neighborhoods, ones that haven't been taken over by yuppies doing renovations. We're looking for homes with folks who have lived in there a long time, preferably all their lives. Because the longer they've been there, the better the chances are that they've accumulated a lot of stuff.

The way a person keeps up their outside property can tell a picker a lot about what the situation might be like on the inside of their house. If there's paint chipping off the house because they never paint it, or they have things piled up in the yard—rusted cars, old farm machinery, building materials—chances are they'll have a lot of things piled up in their living room. Another way we know that a house might be full is when we see a window with yellowed or bleached-out curtains smashed up against the panes; in a lot of cases, this means there are piles of stuff pushing up against them that have been there long enough for the sun to fade the fabric. In older properties, where things have been left alone for a long time, you see this a lot.

Extra buildings are other things we look for. When we see a property with several big old outbuildings, like sheds or barns, chances are the owners are storing cars or old farm machinery—things we might want to buy. If the building has been overgrown with tall grass and weeds, then we know the stuff inside has been sitting there untouched for years, maybe decades. Score!

Unbelievably, we pay close attention to paint colors. We keep our eyes peeled for homes painted all those weird colors they used in the 50s—avocado green, harvest gold, pink. If the person who lives there hasn't gone to the trouble of updating them, you can be sure they've let other things—like cleaning out their attic or basement—slide as well.

THERE ARE SOME definite deal-breakers when it comes to finding picks on a free-style mission. If we see an aboveground pool, a really neatly manicured lawn, a brand-new truck or shiny John Deere tractor in the carport, or plastic kids' toys in the driveway, we just drive on by. Those things make us think that the people who live there are younger or that the residents are into making upgrades. All their stuff has been sold at a yard sale or was donated to a thrift store.

Sometimes these people get in touch with us via one of our ads, claiming they have things we'd want to buy, which, of course, they probably don't. This is a prime example of why we have to ask so many questions on the front end when we're vetting possible stops on planned picking trips.

Another thing to consider on the road: zoning laws, which define what a property owner can and can't do with their property. Some of the terms directly affect how well we can do our job, like the codes that dictate how many outbuildings a property can have and how large they can be; how tall you can grow your grass; and those that limit what a homeowner can put out in their front yard, which usually means dilapidated cars and other nonworking vehicles—things that we specifically look for when we're out free-styling.

Zoning codes aren't federally mandated, so different states have different rules. The same goes for cities and counties: each is governed by a different set of zoning codes, which means that the landscape can change pretty quickly. You may be driving down a road in a county lined with properties filled with outbuildings with failed paint jobs, which are surrounded by weeds and cars up on blocks—those *Dukes of Hazzard*–looking places are a beautiful sight to a picker—and then, without warning, find that the view out the window looks like an episode of *Leave It to Beaver*, all neatly manicured lawns and perfect-looking houses right over the city limits. Strict zoning codes are what we call a style-cramper—a thing or event beyond our control that gets in the way of having a good pick.

When you're in an area with tough codes, it can be hard to see the clues you need in order to figure out if you've come upon a solid place to pick. With nothing in the yard, you might drive by the mega-pick to end all mega-picks and you'd never know it.

If you don't want to chance driving into no-visible-junk territory, check in with the department of planning in the area you want to pick and ask them what the deal is. Another way to get around zoning issues is to just not go free-styling in those areas; use other methods to pick there, like ads in papers or the Internet.

WE USED TO spend all the time we weren't on the road on the phone, following up on leads we found in newspapers and trade journals, on the Internet, or from tips from people we met along the way. That all changed a few years ago, when Mike hired Danielle.

These days, she makes all the calls that we used to have to make ourselves. Having her on our team saves us a lot of time on the front end, but it can be frustrating when she sends us on a wild goose chase.

It's not always her fault when that happens: her job is really hard. To someone watching our series, finding good properties may look easy; it's not. Danielle spends hours on the phone every day, tracking down leads. While we're out driving around, she stays back at Antique Archaeology, researching stops for our next pick and making contacts for us along the way:

My job at Antique Archaeology is pretty extensive. I run the shop. I do PR. I deal with visitors on a daily basis. I clean and sometimes repair items the guys bring home from picks. I do all the sales.

But, mainly, I'm what you would call a tracking dog. I hunt down and sniff through thousands of leads that come in each year via e-mail or phone calls. My goal is to follow up on twenty of them a day. Sometimes I fall short of that—hundreds of people come through the Antique Archaeology store every week to shop, so they keep me busy—but usually I manage to make all those calls. Of those, I aim to come away with five great leads for the guys to consider.

I search the Internet for leads, too; I look for blog postings about sales, check out bulletin boards on collectors' sites and online classified ads in the cities they plan to hit on their trip. We try to come up with a travel plan for them well in advance so that I can call the Chamber of Commerce in the towns on their route. I call up and ask who the junkers in town are, or who has interesting things sitting around in their yard. I've gone as far as to ask who has city ordinances against them because they have too much stuff all over their yards. People are really helpful, especially in smaller towns.

When I'm following up on phone leads, my spiel changes from call to call; each case calls for different questions, depending on what they have. But usually I start with something like, "Hi, this is Danielle from Antique Archaeology and I work for a couple of gentlemen who collect and resell vintage items. I hear you have a bunch of old bikes on your property. Are you willing to sell any of them? We'd love to see what you have." If they say yes, I ask about specifics— most important, the make, the model, the year it was made. I ask about the condition and how long the person has had it in their possession—basically, I try to find out as much about its history as I can. Finally, I find out if they want to sell and, if so, what they want to sell it for and set up a time for the boys to stop by.

I've found that you don't have to be a walking encyclopedia of collectibles to do my job, but when you're making cold calls on the phone, it really helps to know something about the

items the client has for sale. Sometimes you can find out all
you need to know with a quick Google search. Being able to
have a conversation in which you ask intelligent questions
and have the owner educate you a little bit makes them feel
like a partner in the whole process; it takes them off the
defensive.

In a lot of ways, her job is tougher than ours is. Getting out on
the open road and meeting new people, seeing their stuff and then
learning their back-stories—that's a blast, and it's why we love what
we do so much. Danielle shoulders the weight of making sure our
time on the road pays the bills. And she's great at it.

NINE TIMES OUT of ten, we walk away from a pick disappointed. It's
pretty easy to get discouraged.

But then, some days, the Picking Gods smile on us and throw out
a gimme. For example, we'll see a "For Sale" sign on a car sitting in
the front yard of a property that has all the makings of a mega-pick.
A sign like this is one of our favorite things to see when we're out
free-styling. It means no one's going to be surprised if you walk up
and knock on the door. There's no ice to break, 'cause the sign did it
for you.

It's true, a lot of the time we don't even care about the car: we're
just faking interest in it as a way to get access to the rest of the property. Of course, when you first go to the door, you've got to play
along and ask about the car. But after that, the field is wide-open.

Usually, it's not that easy, though. Most of the time, we have to
work really hard to make cold calls work for us.

When we cruise into a town we've never been to, without any
solid leads, our number-one source is people who have longstand-
ing roots in the area. There are still towns out there where everyone
knows everyone else's name if not their entire life story. Going to

the post office is still a major social event in some of these places. If you find someone who loves to talk, you're in business.

Town squares are a good place to find leads. If there's a main café, we go there for breakfast or lunch and make conversation. Or we just introduce ourselves to the guy sitting on the bench outside the court-house, tell him what we're looking for, and ask if anyone he knows might be able to help us. For the most part, everyone we meet is friendly and helpful. In a lot of the small towns we visit, people don't think it's weird if a stranger tries to stop them to ask a question. If we do run into someone who gets their back up about us poking around, we give them one of our business cards to show we're legit; if that doesn't work, we respect the person's privacy and leave them alone.

When we meet folks who are willing to share info with us, it's game on. We make a point of asking if there are any interesting prop-erties nearby—maybe an old factory or a junkyard, or even a jail-house; we picked one of those in St. Joseph, Missouri, one time.

That's the way we found the Bushkill Amusement Park that was featured on *American Pickers*. We were in Eaton, Pennsylvania, at an antique store. We asked the woman behind the counter if she knew of any unusual places around that we needed to check out. "Well, there's an amusement park. It's been closed for several years. No one's been in it for a while. But I hear that the owner wants to sell some of the stuff left there so he can afford to get the park going again." It was a classic case of a picker being in the right place at the right time.

Bushkill originally opened in 1902, so a lot of the equipment and props were really old. The best part of the day was running around inside the funhouse, which is the oldest in America. (Who says pick-ing is all work and no play?) We ended up buying some great sideshow banners that were almost as old as the park.

The amusement park is a great example of us getting a lead on a mega-pick by asking a local for advice. But sometimes we don't even have to ask anyone to find what we're looking for; it's right there, staring us in the face.

SIDESHOW BANNERS

Self-taught artists in the early and mid-part of the last century painted colorful images of acrobats, clowns, performing animals, and carnival freaks on large pieces of canvas that were used as promotional signs for sideshows and circuses.

In small cities, active downtowns are becoming a thing of the past. Since the 1970s, we've all seen businesses that used to have a presence on a courthouse square either close or move out to the mall. This has left some amazing buildings unoccupied—well, unoccupied by people, that is. Lots of stuff gets left behind in these big moves.

If we see a building that looks promising, we stop and see if the owner is around, or look for a caretaker. If no one is around, we find the closest open business and see if they can give me the owner's name. Sometimes they'll lead us right to him; other times, we'll spend a whole day searching.

That happened to us in Memphis not long ago. We found this amazing eight-story brick building downtown, which still had the original "Memphis Cycles" sign outside. It was packed with unopened boxes of bike and motorcycle gear dating back to the 60s; you could see all the bikes and the tables in the back piled high with new-old-stock, a term pickers use that applies to items that were ordered in bulk by the store but were never sold or used once they arrived (the abbreviation we use for it is NOS). There were tires, fenders, lights, seats, rims—just boxes and boxes of it, sitting there, taunting us through the smudged glass window. Nobody came to the door when we knocked; it was obvious no one had worked there for a long time.

So, we went across the street to a deli and asked the guy at the counter if he knew the name of the owner. He gave us a name and number. First, we tried calling the guy, but he didn't pick up. So we got his address and went to his house right away.

It was the wrong guy; we got bad info. But we still had visions of dead-stock bike gear stuck in our heads, so there was no way we were going to give up. We knew the stuff in that building was worth it if we could just get inside.

Our next step was to go to the local tax assessor's office and ask them to look up the real owner's name and address. But this time it was early afternoon. After calling this guy and getting no answer, we went to his house. Nobody home.

We had run out of options. After six hours of searching, we decided to drive by one more time before giving up.

This time, someone was there. The owner had unlocked the door and was poking around inside. Just our luck—he wouldn't even let us in the front door. After all that trouble, he wouldn't sell anything.

One of the reasons for this was that the building and all the stock was owned by him and his two brothers, and they couldn't agree on what to do with the place. One brother wanted to sell it, while another thought that was a bad idea: the business had been in their family for three generations and it was hard for them to let go.

The guy who opened the door for us was the only one of the three who had stayed in Memphis, so he became the caretaker by default. He had mixed feelings about getting rid of the contents, too; the store had been closed for years, but he still felt a responsibility to his father and grandfather, who had started the business. Memphis Cycles had been a big part of all of their lives and it was hard to let it go.

OFFERING LEADS IN EXCHANGE FOR DEALS

One of the oldest tricks in the picker's Bible is trading a hot lead for a better price. If you're trying to buy from a stubborn collector or dealer and happen to have a juicy lead about a piece they might like, swap it for a nice discount.

PICKING 101

. . .

WE'RE CONSTANTLY BEING asked, "How did you buy that? How did you get that grouch to let you in his house?" And you know what we say? We asked. Sometimes it's just that easy.

We're not special: every picker out there has the same chance we do entering a new pick. Any one of the thousands of other professional pickers out there can get inside a house just as quickly as we can. It's as easy as a knock on the door.

Because it is such a simple process, we always have to be aware of what our competition is up to and to follow what is known among people in our industry as the Picker's Code, unofficial rules of conduct that a picker should follow when he's out on the job. The Code is a casual agreement and not enforced by any organization, but if a picker flat-out breaks its unspoken rules, he'll pay with his reputation and access.

First of all, know that the Code doesn't apply to people who are casual collectors, weekend yard-sale shoppers, and other nonprofessionals like that: it's aimed at those of us who do this as a business and who buy from private clients that we find via research, references, and door-knocking. In other words, you can pick to your heart's content at retail or resale stores or temporary situations like estate sales or flea markets without stepping on anyone's steel-toed boots.

Pickers travel a lot, so the places they pick are always changing. But most professional pickers have a home base, which becomes associated with us and is considered our domain.

Basically, any property that the home-court picker "discovers" and manages to develop a solid relationship with the owner with the intention to pick (whether a sale has actually happened yet or not is, surprisingly, beside the point) falls into his territory. The size varies from picker to picker: it might be a single street in a small town or it might span an area that crosses state lines. Not every city or county necessarily ends up being claimed by a picker; places that don't "be-long" to anyone are fair game to any picker who comes driving down the road.

With all that said, the big question here is pretty obvious: how does a picker know if a property he comes across while he's out on a free-styling trip belongs to another member of our tribe?

Well, if the picker is new to the business, he probably doesn't have any way of knowing which houses and farms and junkyards have already been claimed by another picker. It's only the guys who have been doing this for a long time who know that kind of thing—and, honestly, because they're the ones with the sharpest eyes and know how the business works, those pickers are the only ones most of us are concerned about, anyway.

Even pros in-the-know land on another picker's property. When this happens, you just have to use your best judgment on how to proceed and be careful not to burn any bridges. You have to be fair and respect the Code, while still standing up for yourself.

This kind of thing happened to Mike a few years back in New York:

I got this lead from someone I met at a swap meet up there. The owner of the property had a lot of old motorcycle gear, as well as a bunch of other cool things, like industrial light fixtures and old Civil War relics—just a lot of different collections. He used to sell at flea markets, so there was a lot of diversity there. I had initially called him just to follow up on a motorcycle he was selling, but we hit it off on the phone, so he let me come over.

I had been there for several hours, picking away, with my van parked out in front of the seller's house. I had put a bunch of stuff I was interested in sitting out into the driveway; it was obvious something was going on.

All of a sudden, a truck rolls up to the house: it's another

*picker, a local guy. He gets out of his truck and walks up to
me. He was really irritated and got all up in my grill and everything: "What are you doing here? Why is some picker from
Iowa working on my turf?"*

*I kept really calm and tried to convince him to be rational
about what was happening. I asked him what he was interested
in finding here.*

*"Victrolas—I know for sure this guy has a bunch of old
record players in his attic. I've been working on him for years,
trying to get him to sell, and then you walk in and he opens up."*

*You know, that's not my fault: I just happened to be in the
right place at the right time. I didn't know the seller had been a
picker target for years.*

*So, I say to the other picker, "Okay, I know it's your
territory—and I respect that. But I did get in here first. So
here's the deal: you get all the Victrolas—I won't buy any of
them. But I get first option on everything else."*

*He wasn't thrilled but he knew it was fair—plus, I was
headed back to Iowa the next day, so it wasn't like I was the
new threat to him. So, everything turned out okay. Everyone
went home happy.*

IT'D BE NICE to be able to say that, as pickers, we follow our gut
every single time. But that's just not the truth: there are places that we
have to pass by a million times before we slow down. Usually, when
we do finally get around to stopping, the owner will say the words
every picker dreads hearing the most: "I wish you'd been here a
week ago . . ." He's just sold the exact things you're looking for.

The moral of this story is that if you think a place looks even half-
way good, then stop. What's the worst thing that's going to happen?
Someone will yell at you and tell you to get off their property? Well,

then say thank you, get in your car, and go on down the road. No big deal: there's always another pick waiting.

Or you hand them your numbers and a flier listing what you're looking for and maybe they'll call you later. Or maybe they'll pass it on to their neighbor and he calls you. That's the way picking works. It's all about building relationships.

2
THE PICKEES

THE PEOPLE PICKERS MEET ARE A BREED ALL THEIR OWN

THERE ARE SO MANY PEOPLE WE'VE MET
WHILE SHOOTING AMERICAN PICKERS
THAT I'D LOVE TO GO BACK AND SPEND
MORE TIME WITH. TURN OFF THE CAM-
ERA; SIT DOWN ON THE COUCH, POP OPEN
A COLD DRINK, AND JUST TRADE STO-
RIES FOR A FEW HOURS.

—Frank Fritz

Picking takes us on a daily treasure hunt. We're constantly coming across amazing finds and learning new things and we get to hold pieces of American history in our hands every day. It's really kind of amazing.

The biggest surprise is the way people live. It can be kind of scary at first, to be honest—the shock of the surroundings. Our picks are usually not mansions. But after you sit down and start talking to the owner and get to know him, all the stuff around you disappears. You can be sitting in a pile of dirt and still have a great conversation with someone.

It's definitely the people who make our job worth it. Getting to meet new folks and hear their stories at every stop are the biggest perks in our line of business.

You can say that our job is like going on thousands of blind dates every year. And just like on a blind date, we can tell within five minutes if we have any kind of spark with a seller. If there's no chemistry—no easy back-and-forth, no friendly joking—then chances are the pick's not going to go very well. If you don't jibe with someone personally, chances are your professional relationship isn't going to be that hot, either.

When this happens, it's usually best to just cut your losses, politely say good-bye, and walk away. It's just not worth the energy, time, or the hassle to work on winning them over. (This all goes out the window, of course, if they've got something really amazing that you see on the property, something you've just got to have. In that case, you might want to suck it up and try to slide on through the all-important buttering-up process.)

Lucky for us, most people are happy to see us and act as though they've known us forever. Sometimes we're so in sync with the person we're picking from that we go back and visit them again and again. And a lot of the time, those return visits won't even be about the pick: we honestly like the person so much that we make the effort to have a proper visit with them—drop by for a beer and just talk about junk. Or life. Or both.

We've met people on picks who have become like family to us. Take Judy in Ohio, who's been on our series a couple of times. She's like our grandmother! Right off the bat, we felt at home with her and vice versa; that's why she let us come back to pick her eight-story factory building, where she has dozens of collections, including major WWI propaganda posters. Heck, she even made us cookies. When it comes to picking people like Judy, buying is secondary to the relationship we're building.

That said, we're pickers. We've gotta make deals to survive. If we spend too much time socializing, we lose valuable picking time. We have to make sure not to get too comfortable in one place for very long. If we want to pay the rent, we have to eat our cookies, say our farewells, and move on to the next honey hole.

WE DIDN'T INVENT the wheel when it comes to free-style picking. Pickers have been knocking on doors since the beginning of time. But, then, a lot's changed since the beginning of time.

Today people are so worried about crime and violence that they have their guard up—for good reason: the world is a more dangerous place than it was forty or fifty years ago. People used to leave their doors unlocked all the time, never worrying that a stranger might walk in off the street and steal something. In most places, that hasn't been the case for years. So, to younger people, who were always taught to be wary of any stranger, having someone they don't know knocking on their door seems weird. But guys who are in their seventies and eighties get it; they grew up in a time when this kind of thing was okay.

During the early and middle part of the last century, people had service workers coming to their doors all the time, especially if they lived in a rural area where there weren't many stores. The milkman would stop once a week; then, every few months, the vacuum cleaner salesman would make a call, or the Bible guy would stop by. It was a social thing for them.

Many of the homes we pick belong to older folks—they've had more years to accumulate things and they're more comfortable with people coming up to their door and wanting to talk. Some of these guys even tell us they used to go "door knocking" themselves back in the 40s and 50s.

But no matter what the age of the property owner is, the sad truth is that most of the things we come across on picks we can't buy—and we're talking 75 to 80 percent of what we see. The odds are against us.

Why? Most of the time, if there's a lot of obviously great stuff rusting out in someone's front yard or sitting in an old, abandoned storefront, covered in dust but in plain sight, it's there for one reason: someone still wants it around.

A good example is the owner of Memphis Cycles—he wouldn't even let us step through the front door of the former motorcycle storefront, which was packed with cool bike parts. Guys like him communicate who they are through their property.

We don't fool ourselves by thinking that we're the only pickers in the world. In fact, we're 100 percent positive that dozens of other pickers have talked to this guy way before we found him. And he turned them down, too. That building would have been cleaned out a long time ago otherwise.

And so, the Memphis Cycles guy and his eight stories of awesomeness have become a sort of urban legend to us pickers. It's amazing. We hear guys talking about him at swap meets and flea markets coast to coast: "Hey, have you ever picked Memphis? Did you hit that cycle guy?" "Naw, man. That guy's tough; he never sells anything." "Huh. Well, I heard he let Jersey John inside . . ."

We all share war stories about our experiences with him—the lucky guys who have gotten through the door get bragging rights while the rest of us hold on to the dream that someday we'll be welcomed inside the inner sanctum, too. Man, pickers fantasize about guys like the Memphis Cycles dude like he's a rock star or something. And we're the crazed groupies, all trying to get his attention.

But you know what? More power to him. It must feel really good to be somebody's rock star.

OH, THE PEOPLE YOU'LL MEET

In the picking business, you don't meet those rock stars every day. In fact, those guys are just one of the many types of sellers a picker meets out on the job.

We come across individuals and families, introverts and extroverts, collectors and other pickers. And each of these groups has certain character traits and habits that it is helpful to know going in.

Before we start breaking those down, let's go ahead and talk about the big elephant in the corner: over-accumulators. They're all about quantity, not quality. Over-accumulators may have major tonnage, but the condition of their things is usually so poor that it's rarely worth our time to stop and look through it.

But the main reason we don't deal with them is pretty simple:

they don't want to sell anything. They won't let anything go; they can't even bring themselves to give up a pan. So why would we bother wasting time with them when there are millions of other sellers out there willing to let us buy—or, as we like to say, pop?

Here are some of the major types of pickees you'll come across on the road who *are* usually willing to make a deal.

The Good Old Guys

The older people we focus on have massive amounts of stuff that they've collected over the years, which is awesome from a business angle—the more we buy, the more we can sell. The biggest bonus of picking older guys is that they usually have some pretty spectacular stories to go along with their possessions; they have history on their side. This information is invaluable to us for a lot of reasons. It helps us sell the piece later (a good back-story is gold when you're selling an item to a collector); it teaches us more about the things we're picking (a good picker is always looking for ways to gain knowledge in new areas; and it gives us a glimpse into the life of the seller—it's like getting a personal history lesson).

We live for guys like Bobby Twig, the guy we featured on the series, who still runs the junkyard in Maryland that his grandfather opened in the 20s and who can basically track down and ID every piece on his property. Same for Will-I Green, the guy who has a White Castle building in his front yard.

RESTAURANT COLLECTIBLES

When restaurants and hotels go out of business, sometimes they liquidate all the dishes, flatware, service pieces, and linens. The most valuable things on the collectibles market are pieces with the name of elite or classic companies that have gone out of business.

One of the coolest things about Will-I's collection is that it is based totally on nostalgia. The dude actually purchased the general store that he used to shop at when he was a little kid! He literally bought a memory from his youth so that he could continue to enjoy it today, right in his backyard. Walking through the store with him was like going back in time; he had so many great memories to share. Guys like Will-I are why we stay on the road.

We get some flack from people who say we're taking advantage of older folks, that we trick them into selling their heirlooms. That's total nonsense. We never want to rob someone of their memories; we can't tell you how many times we actually have to talk people into keeping things that they want to sell but that they've explained have a very heavy emotional history.

We picked a family farm in Fort Worth once, where Mike made a deal to buy a sign attached to the front panel of the barn, which was advertising a roofing company. The logo included a horse's head, which was a big selling point: vintage ads featuring animals are more desirable than those with just words.

After making the deal, Mike walked up to the property's main house, where he met the nineteen-year-old granddaughter of the farm's owner. They started talking and she told him that she was in school for equine studies and that she eventually planned to have a career working with horses:

After I talked to her and found out what she wanted to do with her life, I told the family that I didn't think I wanted to buy the sign, after all: they needed to keep it for the girl to have when she becomes an adult. I told her that later in life, when she had her own farm and her own horses, she'd remember that sign and wish they hadn't sold it.

I told her that the sign might not seem very important right now, but that if her family let it go, she'd regret it later. It was something that had been in their family for a long time; her mother told me that she remembered the sign hanging on the barn when she was a little girl.

Sometimes people don't understand how much something means to them until it's gone. We try to always remember that. If you respect the people you're working with, then you owe it to them to be honest in that regard. We're looking at it from the outside, so we can point out, "Hey, maybe your kid is going to want this someday. Maybe you should keep it."

But the truth is, a lot of people just aren't very sentimental; if they don't sell their family Bible to you, they're gonna sell it to the next guy who comes along.

It's a different story when it comes to regular, run-of-the-mill stuff like old signage and farm equipment; when some guy has a ton of that backed up in his yard, we tend to think we're doing him a favor by taking it away. If they don't have a family to pass their things on to and don't have an outlet where they can sell it (for folks who may not own a computer, eBay is not an option), someone eventually is going to have to come in and haul the stuff off to the junkyard anyway. We're saving them the hassle.

Yes, we try to make money on these sales; it's how we earn our living. But we're not in the business of tricking people into giving up something they love and cherish and want to keep. We're not out to take advantage of any seller, no matter how young or old they are.

FARM EQUIPMENT

Farm collectibles can be small (hand tools and garden implements) or big (tractors, backhoes, plows), with the value to match. The worth of items will depend on several factors, like where the item is from, how rare or old it is, and what it is (or was) used for. Used pieces of historical value may be worth more than more-conventional items.

The Big Talkers

Pickers, as a rule, are not timid guys; our job description entails a lot of interacting with the people. We like to make friends and really enjoy a good conversation. From time to time, we run across professional talkers. These guys have a story for everything, and it's usually a long one.

As we said before, back-stories are awesome; we love learning about the history of the things we pick. But there's a limit to how much we need to know; we can only absorb so much information about the history of the old Pennzoil oil can sitting on the floor of some guy's barn before we decide to pop. Plus, when the seller won't stop talking, it's hard to make a deal. Big talkers don't recognize this.

You have to be really careful with these guys. You never want to hurt someone's feelings by cutting them off while they're giving you the history of an old oil lantern their great-grandmother used in the 1880s, but pickers can't afford to get stuck in one place for too long, especially if the stuff isn't that great or you get the sense you're not going to be able to buy anything.

The talkers who really get excited when they see us pull up are the hard-core junkers. The fact that someone is coming to them asking about their collection is like their dream come true. They're in heaven. And if you have the time to spend with them, then that's fine—it can even be a lot of fun. But talk doesn't pay for our gas.

OIL, GAS, AND PETROLEUM COLLECTIBLES

Until the late 1940s, oil was pumped from a bulk barrel into a reusable glass bottle. These bottles were often labeled with an embossed brand name. Founded in 1859, Quaker State Oil Company made petroleum products to lubricate steam engines, machinery, and wagons.

When a picker gets in a situation where he can sense the talk will be long and the pickings pretty slim, he has to make a decision. He can do one of two things: cut his losses, say good-bye, and make a break for his car, or stay the course, knowing that at some point they'll run out of steam or the sun will go down, whichever happens first.

Again, this might take a long time. We've worked on people for hours, hoping they'll eventually lose steam and get around to selling. Heck, Mike listened to one junkyard owner tell stories for over ten years before he ever got a crack at picking the best items in his lot.

Investing that much time in one seller is a pretty big sacrifice. You have to use good judgment and listen to your gut during times like this. If your instincts tell you that a payoff will eventually come, and that it will be worth it, keep coming back. Being patient can sometimes pay off, big-time. We ran into a talker down in Mississippi a few years ago, who had building after building of amazing stuff—and a really long story to go with every piece. When we could manage to get a word in, we'd ask for prices on the things we liked; the guy didn't want to sell anything. After three hours of his grand talking tour, Frank was toast:

I told Mike, "I'm done, dude. This tour is over." I went back to the van and Mike stuck it out for an hour more. Then he gave up. Finally, we're both in the van, pulling away, and this guy is literally walking with us, still talking. And right before we really started rolling, he goes, "You guys like motorcycles, right? Let me turn you on to a guy about thirty miles down the road."

And you know what? He sent us to the best pick we had that week. And I had totally given up on that dude; I was done. But Mike kept talking to him. He had the patience and he stuck it out to listen to his stories.

This scenario could be reversed at any time. Some days, it's Frank that has the juice to keep going and Mike that tuckers out—but whatever. This was a time that Mike listened to his gut and stuck it out. In the end, it was worth the headache.

The Junkyard Heirs

When we put out ads looking for picks, we get a lot of calls from grown children or grandchildren trying to help their parents or grandparents unload some of their collections. The kids know that if the stuff in their granddad's five aluminum-sided sheds doesn't move soon, they'll be stuck dealing with the collection of a thousand beer cans later on.

Probably a third of the people we pick are sons and daughters of collectors who have ended up with their parents' stash after their parents passed on. Sometimes the kids are collectors, too, and they're stoked to have a ton of cool new items to add to their stash. Other times, they're minimalists whose nightmare of being willed a dozen barns full of old machinery, gas pumps, and a hundred rusted farm tools has just come true. They see their junk inheritance as an inconvenience and they can be pretty overwhelmed.

BEER CANS

One way to date beer cans is by the shape of their top. Until pull-tab cans were invented, beer cans were either flat-topped (to open with a can opener) or conical. Conical cans were sealed with the same screw-tops used on glass bottles today. Conical-shaped tops were the norm from 1935 through the early 1960s, when pull-tabs were introduced. The first pull-tab can was invented by Mikola Kondakow in 1956. These were commonly used until the mid-70s, when the stay-tabs were introduced. The modern stay-on tabs were invented by Daniel F. Cudzik in 1975, and that style has been popular since the 1980s.

FILM PROJECTORS

The Motiograph projector made by Sears and Roebuck is a very desirable projector, in terms of collecting. They were used to play silent movies.

When the heir decides to lighten the load, it's a perfect picking storm for us: lots of stuff, little-to-no sentimental attachment, and super-motivated sellers. We get there and it's like the moving crew has arrived: load us up and we'll move it on out.

A good example of this is the woman named Michelle that we picked in South Carolina last year. Her dad had recently passed away. He worked as a projectionist and on the crews of several films made in their area, and during his career he'd amassed some really stellar movie memorabilia like box office posters, vintage metal film canisters, camera tripods, and film stills that he stored in a warehouse. There were dozens of projectors and reels from films he'd worked on, like Martin Scorsese's *Cape Fear*. Way cool stuff.

Michelle was really concerned about the volume of what she had to deal with. Plus, she didn't want her dad's treasures going to just anyone. She knew it would be valuable to someone and wanted to make sure that it got into the right hands. We were stoked to be able to buy a lot from her—film buffs like to buy old projectors to use as décor, so we scored big on those—and were happy to give her some names of other collectors who might want to buy the rest. She was in a tough spot and we were glad to help her out.

In the end, she was satisfied with our exchange. She picked up some extra money and got the satisfaction that there were pieces of her father and his work being taken back out into the world.

One final note on picking families: keep in mind that there is always the chance that you'll get stuck in the middle of infighting. Siblings are usually the trickiest to deal with; one kid will want to sell everything so they can cash out, while their brother or sister argues that they need to keep some items for sentimental reasons. And if you're standing there with your wallet out, ready to show them some money, it can be frustrating. Sales don't happen during family feuds, so if you sense one brewing, walk away.

The Couples

It's not just the kids who get left with figuring out how to deal with massive collections in picker families. Junk widows—women who love men who love stuff—are everywhere.

Not a week goes by that we don't run across a couple like Deanna and Boo, whom we met when we were free-styling in South Carolina last year. Their property is full of cars, which are Mike's passion: he was a racer back in the 70s. Some of the cars belonged to his grandfather and father, who were automotive freaks, too.

When we first met them, Deanna and Boo were engaged and going to get married—as soon as they fixed up their house and got rid of some of Boo's stuff, which covered eleven acres. He wasn't necessarily thrilled about selling off parts of his hard-earned collection (and he didn't plan to let go of some things, like the car Ryan Newman drove at Talladega—what hard-core race fan would?), but Deanna was on him to scale down so they could settle down. From our perspective, the timing was perfect: she wanted to move things out and we were there, happy to help.

The one thing we try to remember when we're picking these guys

NASCAR RACER SIGNATURES

According to NASCAR.com, shortly after Dale Earnhardt's death, his signature brought as much as $400 on the collectors' market. Today, the value maxes out at about $200.

(or girls: over-amassing goes both ways, though nine times out of ten it's guys who are being told to lighten up) is that, to them, the acre filled with rusted engine parts isn't junk. People get attached to their possessions; letting go can be a very emotional process. He's worked hard to build his collection and we make sure he knows that we appreciate his dedication and can't thank him enough for letting us take some of it off his hands.

Other Pickers and Collectors

Other pickers are the trickiest sellers we deal with, for a few reasons. One, they know the value of what they have. And they always want you to pay retail. We can't do that; we've got to make money on what we buy and if they're selling to us at market value, we're out of luck. We can only pay wholesale, preferably less.

Two, our fellow pickers know all the signals. They can tell what you're thinking by your reactions, because they get the same kind of reactions when they're picking. They know what a picker's face looks like when he sees something he really likes and they're happy to use it against you. If your face gives you away, then hell, you might as well add 20 percent to the price they had in mind. They know they have you.

Needless to say, we don't make a regular habit of picking other pickers (we don't usually buy from antique malls or flea markets for this same reason). At the same time, pickers don't all pick the same types of things. And if they have any kind of eye, they're gonna have a quality collection. So, at the very least, you can chalk it up to a learning experience, where you let another picker educate you in his specialty.

Neither of us is an expert in, say, early American stoneware pottery or Shaker furniture, but we like the way a lot of it looks and would like to know more about it. So, why not ask the guy who has spent the last twenty-five years of his life devoted to researching Shaker hutch styles from the late 1700s about the kind of joints they liked to use and why. (For the record, Shakers were all about a dove-tail joint.)

Good pickers are like sponges: we want to soak up as much knowledge as possible, whenever and wherever we can. Other pickers offer us a great opportunity to do this.

When it comes to collectors, you have to play picker psychologist. These guys not only ask for retail prices, they're also likely to flip-flop on their decision to sell. That's because collectors rarely want to give their finds up; they may think they do—or maybe someone is telling them they need to (see the "Couples" section above)—but usually they really don't. Why would they? It's hard to build a really solid collection. It takes dedication and work, not to mention time. It's their passion.

Reminds us of a guy named Keith, from Illinois, whom we met through the series. He was a big collector—he had cool early Maytag washing machine products and some wicked cool Evel Knievel toys. He was the one who called Danielle, saying he wanted to downsize—actually, the word he used was "liquidate"—his stash before he made a big move to Tennessee.

We had two main problems picking Keith. One, he wasn't far enough along in his moving process to where he felt pressured to sell; the heat wasn't on yet. (Danielle could have helped us out by asking for a little more information, like whether he had a buyer lined up for his property yet or how long until he was planning to move; the

EVEL KNIEVEL DOLLS

After a major disagreement with the motorcycle-riding daredevil, the company Ideal Toys halted manufacturing of all Knievel products in 1977. EK dolls in original boxes from that era are now worth up to $100.

closer that date gets, the more he'd be willing to sell.) Two, he was still emotionally tied to his things. His brain was telling him to sell but his heartstrings were holding on to everything for dear life. And that's a tough call to make.

What's really interesting to us is when collectors decide they want to be pickers—meaning, they decide they want to buy and sell. They always have a hard time with it, from a sentimental point of view.

The buying part is easy for them; they can already do that with their eyes closed and probably with their hands tied, too. But when the time comes to give up their finds and someone is standing there with their wallet out, ready to buy, things get sticky. Their natural reaction is to pull it away and scream "Mine!" They let the sentimental value of something exceed the retail value. And, from a picker's point of view, that looks like a no-sale.

The Eccentrics

Quirky people have quirky collections—and pickers are all about quirk. Give us the weird, the wacky, the unusual, and we're in heaven. Taxidermy, folk art, and one-of-a-kind pieces are fun to find— remember the cowhide-covered Servel refrigerator Frank picked in Illinois? It was that company's version of a Wunderbar, a miniature fridge model designed in the 1950s that was intended to take appliances out of the kitchen and into other rooms. It's a totally cool concept, made even cooler by the fact that the previous owner had covered it in a printed hide!

We could imagine someone stocking this Wunderbar with beer or other refreshing drinks and putting it in a retro-styled rec room to be used as a combo cooler/serving piece. Though we later found out it was worth as much as $750, Frank was able to get it for $350 during a negotiation that was the most fun anyone had in that city on that day with their clothes on.

Quirky things like the hide-covered fridge sell like crazy. Collectors don't want to buy the same thing everyone else has; they want things no one has ever seen before, let alone bought.

So, we get a huge kick out of meeting guys like Hippie Tom, who had multiples of a lot of things, including bikes, which he hung in the trees on his two-hundred-and-ten-acre property in Wisconsin. Tom was quirky to the core: he had a thing for the number 60 and tried to get the items in his collection to equal that number or a number ending in 60 (160, 260, etc.)—and we're talking weird things, like dustpans and ice picks. Tons of them. Amazing to look at but hard to buy: collectors who have rigid guidelines for their groupings rarely want to split up the gang.

Then there's Butch, the proprietor of the Alabama Museum of Wonder. He had some bizarre stuff—anatomy charts, taxidermy, folk art, old signage, animal bones . . . Butch had it all in his little cabin. He'd made a lot of the things in it himself: he's an artist and uses only things he finds secondhand. He told us his art supply store is the local Dumpster. Awesome.

We can't forget to mention another picker we met, named Ron, aka "The Mole Man." Ron had built an underground house by hand to hold his picks. From the age of fourteen, he dug it out himself, creating rooms twenty-three feet underground, which he reinforced with six thousand two-by-fours (*exactly* six thousand—we find these eccentric guys like their numbers to be exact). There were twenty-six rooms connected by tunnels, each lined with his collection—from wacky light fixtures and vintage signage to his extensive collection of plungers—yes, you read that right: plungers. Ron took one from every house he picked and wrote the date of the pick, the weather that day, and drew a picture of the house on the bottom. Overall, it was like a picker's Disneyland down there—and very weird, but in a totally cool way.

Hobo Jack in Illinois was another trippy pick. Jack was a real-life vagabond—he looked the part, with his long white beard and

the feather stuck in his hat. He traveled for years as a folk musi-
cian, playing harmonica and guitar, filling the time he wasn't
making music as a roving junk collector, something he did for almost sixty years before he settled down at his current property,
which was several acres chock-full of cars, bikes, motorcycles,
and a lot of other masculine junk that makes our picker hearts go
pitter-pat. Frank bought a 1921 Indian engine and transmission
for only $1,150, and Mike scored a pre-1920 Excelsior motorcycle
for just 5 Gs.

The main thing to remember when you're dealing with an eccentric collector is to stay loose. You've got to be really versatile,
and willing to follow their vibe and play by their rules, which can
sometimes be as quirky as the things they collect. But if you can be
patient and try to speak their language, you can take home some
major one-of-a-kind finds.

The Tough Cases

Some people just want to keep collecting; they don't want to get rid
of their things and are not interested in money. These picks are our
biggest challenges.

When you look up "tough pick" in the encyclopedia, there's a
picture of this guy, Danny Bean, that we know. Man, that dude is
one hard nut to crack.

Danny is one of those picking rock stars we talked about earlier.
All the hard-core pickers we know have tried to break through to
Danny: the dude has thirteen buildings full of rusted gold—a major mega-pick, the kind of place we salivate over. We practically
have to change our shirts each time we leave Danny's place, to hide
the drool stains.

The thing that was most annoying about the years leading up to
breaking the ice—*American Picker* slang for the first sale that gets
the picking started—with Danny was that we could see everything

he had right there in plain sight. This place drove us crazy. He'd let us in; we could climb over all the piles of great old car parts and motorcycles and furniture and antique farm equipment, but he'd never give in. You could look—he'd even let you touch. But buy? Never.

Danny lives in Illinois, just a few hours away from Le Claire, so, last year, we made it our mission to convince him to break the ice. Our strategy was easy: we were going to visit him until we became part of his routine. By the time we were finally allowed to pop on something, he almost expected to see us every time he opened his door, standing there on his doorstep: Here we are, ready to buy. Look—we've got cash!

The thing to remember with guys like Danny is that most will sell something—eventually. It might take a year, even a decade. But one day something in their brain will click and they'll just decide to let go a little. (That's a good case for making sure that you leave your info at every stop; you never know when someone will have a change of heart.) And when that happens, it's the picker on the scene when the time is just right that will reap the rewards.

Unfortunately, we know that just because we broke the ice with Danny Bean once doesn't mean he won't freeze back up again the next time we stop by. So we're gonna hedge our bets and keep him in regular rotation. The more we visit him, the better our odds of success.

KEEPING IN TOUCH

We never leave a good pick without two things: contact info for the seller (maybe he has something we want to come back for sometime) and the names of other folks he knows who might want to sell. We make sure to leave several fliers that they can pass around, too.

PICKING 101

. . .

ANOTHER LEGENDARY TOUGH case was Harold, a retired motorcycle collector from Dansville, New York. For a long time back in the early 90s, every picker in the Northeast was trying to pick Harold; they'd been working on him for years—and for years, they all failed. Harold was really moody and set in his ways. No one could get him to budge . . . until Mike came along.

Mike found Harold the same way he found the woman in Winter Park who sold him the Indian: through an ad in the back of an old antique motorcycle journal. This one was from 1965, and had an ad listing a Flying Merkel motorcycle for sale—a very rare thing to find: these things are like the freaking Duesenbergs of motorcycles.

Even though it was almost thirty years after the ad ran, Mike called . . . and Harold picked up:

> I asked him about the Merkel. I couldn't believe it. He sold it just two weeks before I called! (I found out later that Harold sold the bike to a New York picker I know, who bought it from him at a swap meet for $55,000 and then sold it for $100,000.)
>
> The Merkel was gone, but I figured the call didn't have to be a total wash. I was already on the phone, so I might as well chat Harold up and find out what else he might have.
>
> I started with bike stuff. I asked if he had any of the litera-ture that came with the Merkel or any of his personal motor-cycle stuff—old pictures of him riding it or the boots or jacket he wore when he rode. My motorcycle enthusiast clients love to buy these things.
>
> I asked what he did for a living and what his hobbies were. He started to warm up when he talked about running his family's bookbinding business. He worked out of the basement

in the house he was still living in, and had kept all the cool old tools he used for his job. This was all good news.

Harold was a big collector, and had been all his life. When he was a little boy, he started collecting marbles. And then he started collecting comic books. And then he switched to baseball cards. He said he liked sports, so I asked if he used to play baseball or football and if he had any pennants or old trophies from that time. Yes and yes. I just kept listing stuff and he kept saying yes. I was in heaven.

I asked if he still had all of this stuff. He said he'd kept everything—he was his family's unofficial historian and had a lot of older things passed on to him that had been in his family for generations. He had a packed attic and outbuilding.

I was dying, but I tried not to act too excited. I asked if I could come see what he had. He said, sure: "Anytime."

I didn't think twice about what I was going to do after I hung up the phone. I grabbed my keys, picked up a map—this was way before GPS—got in my van and took off for New York. I drove the 750 miles between Davenport and Dansville overnight. It took me thirteen hours.

I waited until nine a.m. to knock on Harold's door. He wasn't exactly thrilled to see me. I think I freaked him out, to tell you the truth. He wouldn't invite me inside. We talked for three hours standing on his front porch.

It took me a long time to gain his trust. When he did finally warm up and let me look inside his buildings, it was better than I could have imagined. The Merkel may have been gone, but the things that were left blew my mind. The first thing I bought was an old kerosene streetlight. After that, it was nonstop picking for three straight days. I got old books, antique tin toys, belt buckles from the Civil War . . . I completely filled the van.

Harold just sat on a milking stool in his yard and watched me the whole time. I don't think he knew what had hit him.

He was kind of amazed at how quick it all happened. He said, "You said you were coming, but I didn't realize it would be this soon."

Never underestimate the will of a picker. Even when he's faced with a tough case, a picker rises to every occasion and explores every opportunity.

We'll drive twelve miles or twelve hundred miles if the pick sounds good enough. Distance doesn't bother us; missing an opportunity, though—that's what's really tough to stomach.

3

BREAKING THE ICE

HOW TO GET INSIDE
(AND STAY THERE)

PICKING IS LIKE BEING A SALESMAN.
YOU HAVE TO HAVE A LOT OF CONFI-
DENCE IN YOURSELF AND YOU HAVE TO
BE WILLING TO KEEP GOING AFTER HAV-
ING A DOOR SHUT IN YOUR FACE. IF
YOU'RE NOT UP FOR REJECTION, THEN
IT'S NOT THE JOB FOR YOU. YOU GOTTA
BE READY TO HEAR PEOPLE TELL YOU
NO—A LOT.

—Frank Fritz

It's wild how we can meet someone and usually within ten minutes we're inside their home looking around, poking through their barn, or pulling things off shelves in their tool shed.

We don't take this access for granted: we're truly honored to be there. But we earn that right. Good conduct on the job is another part of the Picker's Code.

We're not confrontational. We're not condescending. We're not out to screw anybody over. We're just a couple of decent guys trying to make an honest living.

Neither of us is shy—in this business, you can't be. Picking is kind of like working retail, where you're expected to approach people and try to sell them something. Except we're not selling a product: we're selling our experience and ourselves.

There's definitely some psychology involved in picking. It's not something that's really obvious to the seller—or even to us. Through the years, we've just learned that certain actions we take create specific reactions—the old cause-and-effect song and dance. Once we figured out how to use the results to our benefit, our signature way of doing business was born—and so was the field of picking psychology.

Here's a sample of what's on the syllabus for Picker Psych 101.

LESSON ONE: PHONE ETIQUETTE

It's good to remember that your relationship with a seller begins before you knock on the door. How you come across on the phone is as important as how you act when you're standing on their stoop.

Since Danielle is the one in charge of hooking us up with potential picks, she spends hours every day working the phone at Antique Archaeology, tracking down leads for us to follow.

As you can imagine, this has given her some really good insight when it comes to dealing with clients over the phone. Here's her take on it:

When it comes right down to it, in order to do my job you have to be able to read people really well. You talk to a person for the first time and establish what their personality is, figure out what their needs and likes are, and get a handle on their limitations, and you do that within five minutes of meeting them, over the phone. And if you can respect those limitations and stay within the respective boundaries and not assume you'll be their best friend right off the bat, you're going to be okay. Also, saying "Yes, ma'am" and "No, sir" is gold. Old-fashioned manners go a long way in this business.

But, honestly, I don't have much trouble selling over the phone what Mike and Frank do. The difference between those two and a lot of other pickers is that they really, truly love the things they're doing and have a deep appreciation for what they find. They want to know the history of what they're buying and they appreciate that sometimes it's hard for the seller to let it go. They're sensitive.

Most of the cold calls I make are to guys. This isn't some big sexist move on our part; it's totally practical. More guys collect the kind of things Mike and Frank want to buy—bikes and cars and all that cool rusted stuff—than women do. And because I do have to talk to a lot of men, I can't lie: I know that being a woman works in my favor.

I think these men appreciate that a witty, charismatic, educated, flirtatious woman is on the phone wanting to talk to them about the 1930s Harley in their garage. I know for certain that they're a lot less likely to hang up on me than they would be if it were a guy cold-calling them to talk about buying their motorcycle collection. Instead of being defensive—which is the reaction a lot of people have when you call them up and start asking about their property—they'll say something like, "Wait—how do you know about motorcycles?" They're intrigued.

But being a woman doesn't give me carte blanche to say whatever I want. There are definitely things you don't want to say to a client on the phone. Money is the stickiest topic. It's easy for a prospective seller to feel like they're being taken advantage of if someone calls and starts talking about money right off the bat. You can't act opportunistic. If you come into the conversation with dollar signs in your eyes, people get turned off pretty quickly.

You've got to remember that you're dealing with people's memories; yes, this is a business call, but you need to have a certain amount of respect for their collection. Just don't try to impress them with all your knowledge. If you do, you'll come off like a creeper. It's give and take.

LESSON TWO: PICKERS NEVER QUIT

A successful pick depends on so many different factors. At a minimum, you need a willing seller and buyer, the right amount of cash to make both of them happy, and—of course—some awesome treasure to spend it on. It sounds like an easy equation, but for some reason it's never totally easy. It's like the perfect storm has to brew in order for some of our larger picks to take place.

There's a mega-pick we worked on not long ago, which was over twenty years in the making. There was Bill Burch in Missouri, whom Mike discovered when he was out free-styling one day, who lived in a house in the middle of what looked like a giant junkyard surrounded by huge storage sheds. There were car parts everywhere and huge storage sheds on the property. Lots of stuff and all of it good: a mega-pick *and* a honey hole all rolled into one.

Bill was totally set in his ways. For example, he always sat in the same place on his porch swing, with his arm in the same position; he'd worn a groove in the back of the seat, because he'd moved his fingers back and forth along the same place in the wood for so many years. He was like Danny, the tough customer we talked about in the last chapter, but times ten thousand. He had amassed major amounts of cool junk over the years—more than he could ever enjoy or keep track of: there's no way Bill could account for every piece among the hundreds of thousands of car parts, furniture, pots and pans, bikes and appliances that covered his property. His stuff had put a spell on him; he thought it gave him power, so he didn't want to risk letting it out of his sight.

Guys like him don't scare us, though. If anything, we see them as a challenge. So, we made it our job to break the thickest ice and get invited inside those huge sheds. We stopped by to talk to him whenever we were in the neighborhood—which, in picker geography, is about a two-hundred-mile radius (these little trips are how we manage to rack up all those miles on the van every year). Sometimes Bill would be a jerk and other times he'd be nice as hell. If you pulled up and he was sitting on his porch swing, you knew you had a good chance of finding him in a good mood, because he was already outside. If you had to go and knock on the door and get him to come outside, he'd be all grouchy and that never got us anywhere.

Bill would let us look around a small area of his place, which spanned several acres. And he'd always sell us something small—a spark plug or an old wheel—just enough to keep us coming back for more. Some sellers do this as a control thing: they know that if they give you a little taste of how delicious a pick might be—just let you buy a tiny something that doesn't have a lot of meaning to them or to you—and hold off on feeding you the whole gourmet meal, you'll be back for another taste. They know you don't care about taking home a freaking spark plug—you want to buy the whole car!

From our perspective, popping on something small is a way of breaking the ice. If the guy you're working on isn't budging on the big stuff, it sometimes helps to shoot for an item you know he'll sell—like a $25 oil can or something. Even if you don't give a damn about oil cans—and even if $25 is $20 more than you want to pay—it's worth pulling out the cash just to get everyone warmed up. It lets him know you're serious. Sometimes this works, sometimes it doesn't. But in tough situations, where bigger negotiations stall, it never hurts to try.

Remember that the whole time we were working on Bill, we knew we weren't alone; we knew we weren't the only pickers who'd drive three hours out of their way to find out if he'd finally seen the light and let someone inside one of those massive storage sheds. We weren't the only ones slobbering all over him, trying to convince him to let us at the good stuff.

Mike was there the day of the perfect storm. First of all, Bill was sitting outside on his front porch—a good sign. And it was sunny out—another good omen. Mike walked up, said hi, and boom: Bill goes, "Today I'm going to let you in one of those buildings":

It was everything and more than I ever dreamed it would be.
He was into American cars and bikes, but he also had some

ROLLS-ROYCE

The world's oldest surviving Rolls-Royce sold at auction for $7.3 million in 2007. It was only the fourth vehicle built by Charles Rolls and Henry Royce, who produced their first in 1904.

rare European ones—Rolls-Royces, Alfa Romeos, and really rare British and German motorcycles.

I've picked from lots of guys his age and have found that they picked up a lot of what they know about foreign cars when they were over serving in World War II. They brought that wisdom back to the States with them and then applied it to their collections. So, this stuff was good. It may not have been in the best condition, but it wasn't junk, by any means.

I went back several times after that. (In most cases, we stop after a triple-pick: if you're any good as a picker, you'll be able to get what you need after three visits. Bill's case is different.) He had tons and tons of accumulation.

I'd wander through his junkyard for hours, climbing over stuff and pulling things out of the dirt. Last winter, I bought some old Indian motorcycles from him; they were covered in frozen mud and I had to chip them out with a pick—nerve-wracking. But so worth it. Actually, I am still buying stuff from him.

Besides the power trip we assumed was keeping him from selling, we never found out why, after twenty years of freeze-out, Bill finally thawed the day Mike rolled up to his house.

Patience and persistence definitely pay off in our business, but when you get right down to it, breaking the ice with some people really is all about timing. For some reason, at that exact moment, he decided he was ready to sell. Maybe it was his age—Bill was getting on up there in years. Maybe he had just gotten a big bill he needed to pay, or possibly someone—a family member or even his city or country codes commissioner—was forcing him to sell some of the bulk of his accumulation. But the truth is that Mike was in the right place at the right time; it he'd pulled into Bill's driveway the day before or the day after, the exchange might not have played out the same way.

LESSON THREE: THE POWER OF THE WRITTEN WORD

Pickers are like Boy Scouts without the uniforms and cool badges: we're always prepared. We go in to each pick with a plan. We make sure to have specific talking points in mind before we knock on the door, so that we can dive right in after we introduce ourselves.

You know that sheet of paper that we give to people when we introduce ourselves on the series? That's for real. Everyone we pick gets a one-page flier with our names, the Antique Archaeology logo, and contact info on it—address, cell phone, business number, e-mails, as well as our picking list with the word WANTED in the middle of it. We find this puts people at ease—the idea of two strangers knocking on your door and asking to come root around in your attic is still a hard concept for a lot of people to wrap their heads around—and, for some reason, it legitimizes us to people. We guess they just feel better about letting you farther onto their property if they're given a way to track you down later.

Our picking list is pretty long and really covers a lot of ground; we have three columns listing over fifty types of collectibles, from Airstream trailers to early mousetraps (hey, don't knock 'em until you've seen how awesomely cool the design is on them). We put the things we're most interested in finding up at the very top of the first two columns. First up are motorcycles and motor scooters, specifically Vespa, Labretta, and Cushman brands (you don't have to be specific but it helps when you're working with collectors).

VESPAS

Vespa scooters were invented in 1946 by Piaggio & Co. S.p.A. Originally an aircraft manufacturer, Piaggio & Co. was sent searching for new business ventures in the wake of WWII after their factories suffered from bombings and restrictions were placed on former Axis Powers. The crippled state of Italy's postwar economy and transportation infrastructure discouraged Piaggio from entering the automobile market. With the creation of the Vespa, Piaggio was able to address the urgent need for adaptable and affordable transportation. The Italian scooter company has produced 138 versions of its scooter since its launch. The word *vespa* means "wasp" in Italian.

We stuck bicycles up at the top of the second column so they get almost as much play as the motorized things.

We always carry a lot of copies out on the road with us. You never know when you might find a bulletin board at an antique store or community center that's willing to tack it up. And we make sure that the sellers we visit keep a copy for themselves. Hopefully, they'll hold on to it for future reference; after all, if they're not willing to sell that day, maybe next week will be a different story. You want to make it easy for them to track us down.

We know that junkers tend to stick together. So, sometimes we leave them a few copies of our flier and ask them to pass them along to neighbors and friends. You never know whom they might know. We've gotten some great leads this way.

LESSON FOUR:
IT'S ALL ABOUT TIMING

They say that life is all about timing. From a picker's point of view, that's definitely the case.

There are a lot of major collectors who leave huge estates to their families, many of whom simply aren't interested in dealing with the contents of all the steamer trunks piled up in their garage. That's when we step in—carefully.

People die all the time—no big newsflash there. Sometimes it happens in a timely and expected manner; other times, it's a big shock. In either case—but especially in the latter—you want to be extra-sensitive to the sellers, who are probably experiencing some pretty heavy emotions when it comes to parting with things that belonged to someone they loved. You have to tread really lightly when approaching opportunities that come from that kind of sudden loss. You have to be especially sensitive to the seller's feelings. You don't want to give your picking partner high-fives and start doing the happy dance when you trip over a killer high-wheeler bike in an older gentleman's basement the day after his funeral. That's just not respectful.

It's not just deaths that bring on picks. Births, marriages, divorces, graduations, major moves, business closings and downsizings—reasons people decide to sell fall into every category you can think of.

Sometimes people sell because they need quick money to go on vacation or to pay off a school loan. Other times, they've been hurt or are sick and can't enjoy their collections as much as they could when they were healthy. Whatever the case, these are times when people end up with a lot of junk on their hands that they don't need or have to get rid of, stat. And these are perfect opportunities for us to step in and say hey—we're here. We've got some cash. Let us take some of this off your hands.

LESSON FIVE: PICKER DIPLOMACY

A picker has to be very diplomatic when he's looking through someone's possessions. Remember that people are proud of their collections; they've spent a lot of time and money putting them together.

A lot of times, we have to let people show us their collections before we can get down to buying. Collectors can feel vulnerable when they're showing someone new their stash of favorites. When we meet a fellow collector, he sometimes has his defenses up, because he's never met another guy who understands why he feels the need to spend all his free time going to yard sales and auctions looking for valuable John Deere memorabilia. But, to us, it's awesome.

We're collectors ourselves, and we're extremely passionate about a lot of the things we buy. So when we meet someone else who gets really excited about his collections, it's like talking to a long-lost brother or sister. We're, like, "Hey man—this stuff is cool! Where'd you find all of it? Tell us about it." We get where they're coming from; we've been there and bought the T-shirt.

It's funny, sometimes we're looking at a collection and see things that we think are totally mediocre, but the guy who owns them thinks they're the shining stars of his collection. That goes back to showing people consideration: it's not just things that you have to show respect for, but you've got to honor the owner's background and knowledge base, too. Acting like a know-it-all and telling the guy he doesn't know what he's talking about isn't going to get you anywhere. Plus, it'll make you look like a jerk.

For these same reasons, it's worth remembering that prices are always subjective, based on the seller's experience. Your own experience might lead you to estimate a stoneware jug from the late 1800s as being worth $200 while its owner insists it's priceless—like

JOHN DEERE

The four-legged John Deere trademark logo debuted in 1876. In 1912, the logo was changed to a three-legged deer, and has been altered several times since then.

it was handed down to Moses along with the Ten Commandments or something. You could spend an hour arguing with him about it, but what good will that do? Better to just agree to disagree and be on your way. Acting like a know-it-all will get you nowhere. Let him keep thinking he's got a treasure. He's not hurting anyone.

So many of the decisions a picker makes on the job are about plain old common sense and courtesy. We always make sure to respect natural boundaries with the people we pick. There have been a couple of times on the series when we've really blown it in that area.

One memorable pick was a guy named George—a ninety-two-year-old farmer who had been collecting for forty years. He had a big property with several barns with weeds and trees growing in front of the doors—sure signs to us that no one had been in them in a long time. Totally got our juices flowing.

We were on a roll—George was riding around on his lawn mower, leading us to different parts of his property and pretty much giving us full run of the place. We were in picker heaven.

And then we blew it.

George wasn't very mobile—that was the reason he was riding around on the mower—and so, he couldn't follow us to the junkiest parts of his place, which, of course, was where we wanted to be. At one point, we stayed inside his barn, out of his eyesight, for almost an hour—not cool.

When we finally came out to ask him some prices, we knew we'd blown it by the look on his face. All the light was gone. We'd ignored him and he was offended.

A picker should never assume that he has the rule of the roost on someone else's property. It makes the owner feel like he's being taken advantage of. And that's the last thing we want to do on a pick.

Pickers walk a fine line. You want to act professional and knowledgeable, but you never want to come across as cocky or cold. That old saying is true: you really can catch more flies with honey than with vinegar. Being polite and having good manners goes a long way.

LESSON SIX:
THE OLD SWITCHEROO

People change their minds on us all the time. We've had it happen so many times at this point in our careers that we can almost predict the exact moment when someone's brain clicks from yes to no.

The scenario is always the same: we'll be walking along, looking at their things, and all of a sudden, something will catch our eye. So, we dig it out of the dirt where it's been for the last thirty-six years, or dust off the cobwebs that have been there since Roosevelt was in office. The thing might not even be in very good shape, but all of a sudden, the seller falls in love with it again.

Now, he may have just fully admitted to us that he hasn't thought about the thing in a dog's lifetime. And the piece in question could be in crappy shape, all roached out with rust or whatever. But all of a sudden, when a couple of guys from Iowa start telling them how cool it is, they have a change of heart. Our interest sparks a new appreciation in them and all of a sudden, bam! This rusty thing is their new Holy Grail.

People who are moving or downsizing can be pretty tough customers. They might tell us that they've got to get rid of stuff for space reasons—their new place is just not as big as the one they're leaving, or they have to get out of their rented storage unit. If space is the only reason they're selling, they have the tendency to flip-flop on us.

On the phone with Danielle the day before, a man might say that he was certain he wanted to thin out his amazing collection of tramp art, but when we get there and show interest in all the workmanship of the purses that hobos used to make in the 40s and 50s

TRAMP ART

A type of folk art made by hobos and other vagabond types that included "chip-carving" pieces of random wood into geometric objects with a pocketknife.

by folding and weaving the shiny paper wrappers that covered packages of cigarettes (tramp art is so cool!), he starts to have a change of heart. He suddenly remembers the reason they worked so hard to find these cool pieces of folk art in the first place. And he begins to justify why he should just go ahead and keep it.

Problem is, now we've gotten ourselves all worked up about those bags. So, in order to make the sale, we have to switch into damage-control mode. That means gently reminding them that they called us in because they wanted to sell things; plus, the more things we take now, the less they'll have to pay someone to move. And money is a hell of an incentive.

Reconsidering is the seller's prerogative. We're not going to tell them how to carry out their personal business. But the fact of the matter remains that we're in business, too: it's called acquisition.

LESSON SEVEN: PERSONAL HISTORIES FOR SALE

We may talk tough when we're making deals, but the truth is we're big softies. We're not going to buy something from a seller if we think they might end up regretting it down the line—we're talking family heirlooms, sentimental stuff like that. Splitting up people and the objects that make up this family history is just not the way we work.

Then you can look at it from the seller's standpoint. Let's say someone comes to you with a framed, one-hundred-year-old paper copy of a hand-lettered family tree from the early 1900s, and wants to sell it on the spot for cash. You don't have to read that closely between the lines to understand that they're basically saying they don't want anything to do with it ever again. To you, it might seem like a really special piece that should have some emotional value to it, but the truth is they just don't care. To them, it's just something that gets in their way when they're trying to get to the Christmas ornaments stored in the back of the attic.

A few months ago, a guy came into Antique Archaeology with his grandmother's doll that was from the turn of the last century— the late 1800s, early 1900s. He was, like, "What will you give me for it?" Mike told him it was a great family heirloom and that he thought the guy should just keep it. The dude said he had too much stuff and wanted to get rid of it.

From what we can tell based on our interactions with sellers, at least 75 percent of the population seems to feel the same way. They're all that unsentimental.

So, we try to think about it this way: that doll is now in the shop, and we'll sell it to someone who appreciates it. It will become someone else's heirloom. If that guy wasn't going to make it a part of his personal history, someone else will make it part of their own.

Guess it's kind of a sad story, but it does have a happy ending. And that guy was right about something: the doll was just sitting in a box in his attic, not doing anyone any good. At least, this way she's back in circulation, making someone happy.

LESSON EIGHT:
THE FRAGILE SELLER EGO

Pretty often, we'll come across items on picks, which we want to buy, that aren't for sale—we've figured out that something like 70 percent of the things we want to buy aren't available to us for one reason or another. There are times when we are 100 percent certain right off the bat that the motorcycle we want to buy will never be for sale, no matter how much time we spend working on the owner. Other times, the owner gives us a little indication that maybe—someday—he'll be willing to sell. There's usually not a straightforward sign from the seller that lets us know that either of these is true; it's just an instinct you develop after hundreds of picks.

When this happens, we figure out a contact strategy. These change from person to person, case to case. But they all boil down to human nature: people like attention. It's an ego thing—we all want to feel needed.

When we're "working on" a client—that's picker shorthand for dropping by or calling them on the phone in hopes that they'll allow you to eventually buy the item you're after—it's like we're trying to get them to go out on a date. This takes finesse, grace, and more than a little mind-reading.

If you call too many times, the seller might get flustered or—worse—annoyed. Then you get served with the old line, "Don't call me; I'll call you." That's code for "the deal is dead." The song is over, and our dance is done.

On the flip side, if you don't pay enough attention to them, they might read it as you losing interest. "Hey—you stopped calling me and I figured you lost interest. So I sold that bike you wanted." When this happens, you always want to go back and figure out where you went wrong—what you said or when you should or shouldn't have made a follow-up call. There's never an easy answer.

A picker has to be assertive but not pushy, authoritative but not bossy. It's a fine line and it's taken us years of practice to figure out our formulas for success, which change from pick to pick. And even now, we still manage to screw up the recipes from time to time.

LESSON NINE: GO THE EXTRA MILE—LITERALLY

Mike finds a lot of business by looking through old trade journals. Just because a magazine is forty-five years old doesn't mean the numbers don't work anymore: why not call up an interesting-looking classified from 1964 to see what's still around? It's paid off for him too many times to count. A few years ago, he found an ad placed by a man in Winter Park, Florida, in the 1970s, listing a 1912 Indian racing motorcycle for sale.

This story of how the sale played out is a great example of how persistence can pay off for a picker when he's willing to go the extra mile:

The owner had died many years ago, but his wife still had the bike. Her husband bought it from a vendor in New York in 1962. It was shipped to him in a crate and he never took it out. He had planned on restoring it but he passed away before he could do it. I called her up and asked her a bunch of questions about it—it was almost too good to be true. I also found out that even after all these years there were still a few dealers who were hounding her about selling it. But she never gave in.

I knew I was the guy who could get her to sell. So, I got off the phone, drove directly to the airport, and bought a plane ticket to Florida. I was in the air twenty-five minutes later.

At this point, I literally only had twenty grand to my name. She'd told me the best offer that had come to the table from a local picker, who wanted to give her ten Gs. I went down there willing to offer her fifteen. I was sure I could get her to pop on that.

So, I go to her house, look at the bike—which was totally hot—and show her the money. And she goes, "Well, that's a nice offer, but I'm not going to take it." She wouldn't budge. "I think I'm going to hold on to it."

I'm thinking, what the hell? I just flew all the way down here! I wasn't leaving without that bike.

So I stuck around and spent some time with her. She was really nice and we talked for hours, sitting in rocking chairs on her front porch. She told me about her husband and we got to know each other a little better.

After a few hours, I thought, Hell—what do I have to lose? I got out of the chair and sat down in front of her, Indian-style. I told her, "You know what? I brought $20,000 down here with me, and I want to spend it on that bike. I don't want to go home without that motorcycle. Let's get crazy and make a deal on it."

And she jumped out of her chair and hugged me and said, "Yes! Let's get crazy!"

I was in heaven. But I was also physically in Florida, without a return ticket. I was so distracted by the bike when I flew down that I only bought a one-way ticket. I had to pay twice as much as I should have to get back home.

Dedication pays off—in Mike's case, to the tune of a $10,000 profit: he sold the bike to a collector in New York City for $30,000.

4
PRIMARY AND SECONDARY SEARCHES

HOW TO STRUCTURE YOUR PICK

WHEN YOU'RE WALKING THROUGH SOMEONE'S PLACE FOR THE FIRST TIME WITH THEM IT'S ALMOST LIKE THEY'RE EXPLORING IT FOR THE FIRST TIME, TOO. THIS IS WHEN I'M TELLING THEM WHAT I LIKE AND WHY I LIKE IT. AND THEN THEY START POINTING OUT THINGS TO ME, TELLING ME THEIR BACK STORIES AND WHY THESE THINGS ARE SPECIAL TO THEM. I'M LEARNING WITH THEM.

—Mike Wolfe

Before we picked for a living, both of us worked in fire prevention and safety for a while. Frank was a fire inspector; Mike was a volunteer fireman.

Back when we were doing these gigs, we never thought of them as a way to gain skills that would help us in our picking career. But they absolutely have.

Frank's job took him inside at least 2,600 private buildings each year for over twenty years—a great opportunity to do some on-the-job scouting for the picking business he was running on the weekends. Being a volunteer fireman gave Mike something more specific: it gave him the vocabulary to explain what we do on a pick.

When I was volunteering, I learned that there was a process for the way firemen led searches of burning buildings. First, there was a primary search, where you entered the property and started looking around for obvious things that seemed out of the ordinary that needed to be dealt with immediately—like open flames, lots of smoke, or people who needed help or had collapsed on the floor. Basically, this search is for things that were out in the open.

Next comes the secondary search, when you take a more thorough look and dig a little deeper. You spend time looking in the not-so-obvious places, like behind closed doors and in crawl spaces.

When we first started filming the series, we'd walk into a barn or a big warehouse or something and I'd start looking around, which is my instinct. The director would see me doing this and go, "What are you doing right now? What do you call this?" It hit me then: I was doing a primary search, but instead of fire hazards I was looking for cool junk.

Believe me, when I was training to become a volunteer firefighter, I never dreamed I'd be co-opting their language to explain how a pick is done! But it really works: the two big stages of a pick and the first steps a firefighter takes to pinpoint the origin of a fire are almost identical. Who knew?

THE PRIMARY SEARCH

Picking is all about speed. This isn't a business for people who are slow. You've got to be super-alert and on your game 24/7, or you'll miss out on opportunities. The things you pick up on in the first few minutes of the pick will define what the rest of your pick looks like.

If there's one point during a pick when being fast is most important it's at the beginning, during the primary search. A primary search begins the minute you walk on to someone's property. Before you ever knock on the door, you need to have done a thorough eyeballing of their yard to see if there are any items there to be picked. This is a good time to take stock of the number of outbuildings. If you determine the place is a good, solid pick, you'll want to ask to visit every space. Taking a mental inventory of what you see allows you to ask about a building if it gets left off the "tour."

There are two phases in a primary search. The first involves determining the areas you'll be allowed to pick. Needless to say, picking a multi-acre spread with big outbuildings and things scattered all over the yard requires a slightly different approach than, say, picking the contents of a single barn or basement.

When we're picking large places, a lot of the time the seller will want to walk us through the whole property before he lets us do our thing. Usually, this takes place on foot, though there are exceptions. Remember the episode of the series when we picked the steel yard in Missouri and the owners, Sam and Stan, drove us around on golf carts? Their storage areas were so big and so spread-out that we were glad to have the ride.

During a property tour—and, depending on how much space you're dealing with, this might be as simple as a walk through the kitchen and out into an attached garage, or as complex as the golf cart excursion we just mentioned—be sure to ask which spaces are fair game and which are off-limits. This will help you prepare your plan of action, which is essentially what the primary search is all about.

While the seller is walking you around, you need to be taking everything in, making mental notes about spaces to hit (good: sheds full of rust and dust) and those you want to skip (places that are too clean and orderly; rarely does junk live there). Once you see all your options, you weigh the evidence, make some decisions, and move on to phase two.

The second half of a primary search happens on a slightly smaller scale. Here you zero in on a very specific area—say, the inside of a shed or barn that someone's used for storage.

When you walk into a barn packed with build-up, it can be overwhelming. There's stuff to see everywhere: on the floor, in the hayloft, hanging from the rafters, on the walls . . . The first thing you do when you walk through the door is give the place a quick scan with your eyes, which are your most powerful tool on a primary search. Speed is really important in this phase of the search—especially if you're with another picker, who's probably doing the same thing.

TOOLS OF THE TRADE

Flashlight: If you can't see it, you can't pick it.

Steel-toe boots: Having a motorcycle crush your toes sucks; these make it suck a little less.

Thick gloves: Good for preventing cuts and getting a grip on slippery things.

Van: Unless you're buying smalls, you need the extra room; plus the added height and flat storage area are really handy.

Cell phone: When you're not in the van, make sure it's with you, charged and ready to go. Buy one of those car chargers and keep your cell plugged in when you're out driving around.

Boxes: Different sizes with strong sides and bottoms and newspaper for packing.

Tetanus shot: Rusty nails are a dime a dozen on our turf. Make sure you get one every ten years.

As we said earlier in the book, the two of us are picking partners, but we keep our business lives separate. Because of this, there's often some friendly competition on picks. We both want to be the first to find the big pick.

For that reason, we've worked out a system: the first one who sees something puts "dibs" on it, which keeps the other one from trying to pop on it until the finder decides to buy or not. It's very simple, in an elementary-school kind of way. But even with that rule in place, we still get antsy when we both walk into a new room at the same time.

We usually take different paths when we pick a place, heading off in different directions, so if there is something amazing, like a 1960s pinball machine or a jukebox, we both have an equal shot at finding them. We let fate decide for us. It may seem like one person gets slighted on the deal, but that's just how fate operates.

The thing that gets us through these picking contests is remembering that there's always going to be another pick tomorrow . . .

and the next day, and the next day, and on and on. We don't sweat it. There are a million mega-picks out there, and everyone has an equal shot.

At this point in the primary search, you're looking for showstoppers—big stuff or things that automatically catch your eye. You have to be thorough. Think of it like you're looking before crossing a busy street: look to the left, look to the right, and then look to the left again. Then turn around and see what's behind you. And then do that all over again; one look is usually not enough.

And don't forget to look up! We've struck gold in the rafters before. People stash stuff up there to get it out of their way. It's a natural place for fishing poles and skis and other long, skinny things to hide. Sometimes we even find furniture balanced between beams or collectible clothes hung up there, way out of the way.

If we're in a space where it's possible to climb up high to get a bird's-eye view of the picking area, Mike's all over that. He's a regular junk monkey, treating big piles of stuff like they're jungle gyms. (We sometimes come across climbable piles inside buildings like factories and big warehouses, but they're usually more common in open spaces like junkyards.) Some picking areas are so big that this is really the only way to see everything.

However you get it done, the primary search is all about getting as many different—and better—perspectives on the job at hand as possible. The idea is to quickly collect this information and then use it to focus your energy so you don't waste time.

At this point, if you're picking an enclosed space, you have to figure out where to start picking. This usually means choosing one side of the room over the other. We find that most of the time the oldest things are farthest away from the main entrance to the space; this is because when the owners started filling up their storage space, they filled the space in the back of the room, away from the door, first. Makes sense.

Similarly, we think of big rooms as layers of storage representing time in a seller's life, with the childhood collectibles stored farther back than purchases he or she made as an adult.

The same goes for decades. We were on a pick in Rhode Island recently, where the seller's father had collected a huge mass of chandeliers. We started pulling one after the other off the top of the pile and you could see the years dropping away: the arty stuff from the 70s, then the Space Age–looking ones from the 60s and 50s, and then you're getting into all that deco from the 40s . . . It was like being in an awesome picking time-machine.

THE SECONDARY SEARCH

How you use what we just told you about the primary search depends on your preferences. Each picker is going to have a different plan of action, based on what they're looking for. Priorities change from person to person. For instance, someone who deals in smalls might want to skip the primary search altogether and go straight to the secondary search, which is a lot more concentrated.

On a secondary search, we are actually physically going through the place, opening doors, pulling out drawers, unlocking trunks, digging through boxes, looking under tables and behind big pieces of furniture. This is where we pay attention to details and look for small items. We break out our flashlights and shine them in corners, up into the rafters, in the back of closets, in big rotten holes in the floor—hey, you never know!

In a primary search, we sometimes use big piles as a vantage point; in a secondary search, we dive right into them. Of course, this isn't always very easy: some of these piles are like rusty spiderwebs: from each angle, they reveal something different. That's why you've got to walk around them and check them out from different points. A five-inch move to the right might reveal something you didn't notice before, like a handlebar sticking out of the pile or the top of an old scale that's thinner at the top than it is at the bottom. (On that note, it doesn't hurt to get down on your knees and look at the scene under the pile, too; you may notice some cool-looking furniture this way that's too short to register from eye level but that you can ID from its legs. We learn all we can about the shape and visual traits of furniture from different eras so we can do this.)

Picks are full of lots of individual moments, good and bad. One minute, you might think you're on the worst pick ever, and that you're not going to find anything. Then you take one step forward and look to your right—and pow! There's the mother lode—a dozen ceramic letters in perfect condition, or something else great like that. Changing your position even slightly can change your entire pick.

This is going to sound totally cheeseball, but it's always important to stay optimistic. Even if you only find one really awesome thing on a pick, it's worth it. Good things are getting harder to find every day; be thankful for what you can get.

How thorough we are during the secondary search depends on what our on-the-spot research and gut instinct tell us the pick has to offer. We're sure that we've missed out on plenty of great items just because we overlooked them on our search. But the truth is that you're never going to see everything; it's impossible. But that doesn't mean we don't try.

Every once in a while, a dream pick comes along, where we're invited to pick a space that has been closed off for several decades from human beings (raccoons and squirrels are another story). With

INDIVIDUAL LETTERS

These come in many sizes and styles—from small plastic interchangeable letters used on signs to large metal and ceramic ones that were posted on buildings to spell the name of the business inside. Today, they're frequently used as decoration.

all the pickers that are working the roads today, these virgin picks are very few and far between, so when they come up, we treat our searches of them like surgery. In those cases, we'll check every single nook and cranny of that joint.

YOU FOUND THAT WHERE?

We'd like to say there is a pattern when it comes to what you'll find in each space you pick, but aside from the obvious—meaning, you're apt to find cars and bikes in garages, tractors and other machinery in barns, etc.—every space is a new adventure in terms of contents. A good picker is ready to deal with both the expected *and* the unexpected; he's willing to look in places that may seem like dead ends, just in case.

Of course, you're gonna find junk stored in drawers and trunks and closets; that's a gimme. But people store things in weird places, like inside broken refrigerators and freezers, or even washing machines; you find smalls—items that are more compact and no bigger than a table lamp—stuck inside pots and pans and in the linings of cushions and rolled up in rugs. People hide things in holes in the floor or wall and push things back into the open part of a nonworking fireplace. It's even worth it to flip over paintings and framed pictures to see what might be on the back; a lot of amateur folk artists back in the day were so poor that they'd use both sides of their canvas. Who knows: there could be a Picasso on the back of that paint-by-numbers copy of the *Last Supper*.

Outside, make sure to go all the way around buildings. Look up high—remember Hippie Tom's tree full of cool old bikes?—and look down low: some farmhouses out on the prairie have underground tornado shelters that sometimes get reappropriated as storage spaces. Check out greenhouses, smokehouses, and gardener's sheds and any other freestanding structures you see.

PAINT-BY-NUMBERS PAINTINGS

These do-it-yourself painting kits hit the market in 1950, with the first ones produced by Palmer Paint Company in Detroit. More than twelve million kits have been sold since then.

We even check inside vehicles that look like they've been sitting in one place for a long time. It's worth a shot: who would have thought that Frank would find rare quart-size oil containers and a very cool vintage cigarette machine at that pick in Kentucky? Buses are actually a pretty good place to keep sturdy things that you don't want to expose to the elements but can't bring inside; they're dry and safe from the elements—much better than having them sitting out in the open. When it comes to picking inside buses, the only drawback for us is getting around in them; we're a little bit bigger than we were in sixth grade, you know?

DIRTY BUSINESS

People confuse pickers with antique dealers all the time. Nothing against those guys, but the whole blue-blazer scene isn't our bag. We don't know a lot of antique dealers who are willing to get as down and dirty as we do. Mud, dust, mold, rust, cobwebs, bird and raccoon crap, dead rats—we deal with that every day. Ruining clothes and generally being uncomfortable isn't an issue for true pickers; it's part of our job description.

Recently, we picked an abandoned house in Florida that had belonged to a motorcycle dealer and which looked really terrible going in. We pick run-down places all the time, but this place put a lot of them to shame. It was totally dilapidated; there were holes in the roof where it had caved in and dozens of buckets sitting around everywhere. They were doing absolutely no good: there was water coming in from every angle. The owner's son had just let the place get out of control after his dad died a few years before.

He raced big-time bikes in the 30s and 40s, and when he died, he left his son with some amazing memorabilia. So, we knew there was a good possibility that there would be things still hanging around from that era.

The guy's son told us that other pickers had stopped by before, but that they never even made it in the door; it just looked too far gone. But we were, like, well, we're here; let's check it out. So we rolled up our sleeves and dug deep through the wet and muck to see if this moldy house was a honey hole in disguise.

It wasn't an easy process. Everything in the house had been affected by water. The wooden furniture had swollen so much that the drawers wouldn't slide out, so we asked the guy if we could break into some of the bigger pieces to see what was inside.

Mike cracked open a dresser beside the bed and found a stack of thick plastic bags with water pooled on top; whatever was inside appeared to be fairly well-preserved. He peeled open the first bag, and the sweetness started pouring out of this honey hole: there were dozens of pieces of very collectible motorcycle literature—catalogs and manuals from old bikes, which collectors love to have in their collections. Amazingly, they hadn't totally rotted away. At the very bottom was a bag that held his wool racing jersey from the 40s that had "Indian" stitched in felt letters on the front; he'd raced Indian motorcycles back in the day. It wasn't in the best of shape; moths had gotten to it, and it was falling apart in places, but Mike loved the history of it. To him, it was a treasure, even at $200.

We started that pick with super-low expectations; all we expected to come away with was a few good stories about the guy's father's racing history. But we took a chance and it ended up being one of our best picks ever for old racing gear.

Really, the willingness to take a chance is, to us, the biggest difference between pickers and antique dealers. Pickers go deeper and get dirtier. We're willing to take a shot at the places where there appears to be a .0001 percent chance of success, because we know from past experience that it can pay off in terms of sales. And when you do find a treasure, having an awesome back story of how you found it is the cherry on top of the banana split.

As for the dirt, that stuff washes off.

GET TO KNOW YOUR SELLER

The Florida racer's story is a good example of how important it is to get the history of owners of the place you're picking. Besides the whole social aspect of getting to know the seller, collecting some of their background really helps when you're trying to get a handle on what their property might offer.

Take the son of the motorcycle dealer: if he hadn't told us what his dad did in the 30s and 40s, we probably wouldn't have stuck around, let alone taken apart his bedside table.

It pays off to do a little sleuthing at the beginning of a pick. You just poke around a bit—it's the detective part of our job—and ask about the owners' job history, their hobbies, clubs they belong to now or did in the past . . . Were they a scout as a kid? Maybe they still have some of their vintage uniforms and badges packed away in their attic; if it's old enough, scouting gear can be worth a lot of money. Were they a Freemason or in some other organization that required them to buy uniforms or equipment that might be worth something to a collector? All you've got to do is ask; that's not hurting anyone.

Obviously, we have pretty specific questions when we're trolling for insider info. If we're talking to an older guy, we want to know about his childhood and his career. We want to know what he did

MASONIC COLLECTIBLES

There are countless Masonic collectibles on the market, from jewelry to furniture. But don't expect to buy directly from Masons or Shriners: they are not allowed to sell props and memorabilia for profit.

Freemasonry's origins are a matter of debate, though early Masonic lodges were definitely in existence in Scotland in the late 1500s. Today, there are an estimated six million freemasons all over the world, with about two million in the United States alone. Masons have been persecuted at different points in history and are often the target of conspiracy theories. Despite some anti-Masonic sentiments, several important American politicians, including George Washington, had been Masons. Today, Masons are widely involved in charitable and community-service activities throughout the country.

for a living; a retired salesman might still have cool leather brief-cases stuck in the back of the closet, while mechanics probably held on to tools and gas and oil collectibles, something that always brightens Frank's day. We want to know how he got around when he was younger: did he ride a bike or drive a car? Does he still have them anywhere? And, if so, can we see them? You get the idea.

One question leads to another, and with each answer you get more and more clues to help you on your pick. Not only that, but this bonding time with a seller can be really heartwarming and inspiring. We learn things about people that we'd never know by just passing them on the sidewalk. You are getting to know them through their possessions. It can be heavy stuff, but it's what keeps us going.

ANOTHER BENEFIT OF asking a lot of questions at the beginning of a pick is finding out where the items came from. We find that people who have inherited or personally collected their stash are usually willing sellers. Dealers—as we've said before—can be a bit of a challenge.

But the folks we really want to watch out for—in addition to the people we determine don't have anything that's old or cool—are the ones who like to buy in bulk from auctions. There's a whole group of guys out there who go around to auctions and buy everything that's left at the end of a sale for one low flat price. If someone tells us that this is how they went about building their collection, it's a huge red flag to us. These guys may have a lot of stuff, but it's not the good stuff; someone else already bid and won that.

On the flip side, if we sometimes find ourselves walking blindly into a picking situation where the owners are planning to have their own big public sale, we have to switch gears a little bit. That's part of the Picker's Code, too: you don't want to totally cherry-pick their stash and then split—like, "Have a good auction! Make lots of dough! We'll just be leaving now with all your best pieces!"

We never want to leave someone prepping for a sale without any good stuff to draw customers in. In order to get folks through the door, you have to advertise some marquee items. We know what sells; we know the pieces that will attract high rollers to their sale. And if we take all of the primo stash, there'll be nothing to lure them in, and the sale's a bust.

At the same time, we're not going to just walk away without anything if there's good pickin' to be done. But we try to be careful and sensitive to the needs of the sellers. We may end up taking a few great things—like, two of the group of four porcelain license plates from the early 1900s that they're selling for $25 a piece but that we know are worth at least $100 each. Or we'll buy all four for more than they're asking, maybe give them $200 instead of the $100 that someone would pay for the group the next day. Anything to keep our picking karma in check.

METHODS TO THE MADNESS

When we're faced with big properties, we look for patterns—otherwise known as the method to the seller's madness. There was a guy named Vic we picked in Louisiana one time, who had acres of bike stuff. After we looked around for a while and had ID'd a few brands and eras of bikes, we realized that he had separated them all by country and type of motor—here's the Japanese motorcycle section, and then behind it is the American bike section. Then over here is where the 1920s car area begins and behind it is the 30s and then the 40s . . .

The guy was giving us some pretty major prices on the things we were finding inside these category lines. So, Frank made it his mission to find out where the things were that weren't organized, his thinking being that if he didn't care enough about the stuff to classify them, then maybe they were not as valuable to him. It was a great concept—and it worked. Instead of trying to buy something that the guy cherished and kept in a place of honor, he looked for the items that seemed to be out of order. He ended up popping on a Royal Crown cola thermometer—a really neat piece of advertising that he found stuck behind a rusty shed—for only $30; later, he found out that the thermometer was valued at twice that amount.

We use a version of that idea pretty frequently. People take the best care of the things that they value the most—that's just basic common sense, as is assuming that the things they value the most will cost the most if they agree to sell them. We want to see what's out in no-man's-land; that's where all the deals are.

Unfortunately for us, most people aren't nearly that organized; their good stuff is piled on top of their bad stuff with all the midrange crap scattered everywhere in between. Most of the joints we pick are just a huge mess—a mess that sometimes appears to go on for days. Hell, you can get lost on some properties we've seen. You almost need to pull a Hansel and drop breadcrumbs to find your way out of some of our junkier picks.

DANGER!

We get asked if picking alone is a good idea. Despite the two decades that he spent picking alone, Mike has a pretty strong opinion on this:

Heck no, it's not safe! I wouldn't recommend picking alone to anybody. In fact, I was scared a lot of times when I worked alone.

I was pretty careful, though. When I was out in the middle of nowhere, and there seemed to be no need to lock my van—like, who's going to break into it in rural Kentucky? It's not like it's parked on the street in downtown Chicago or something—I'd make sure to lock it anyway. I'd keep the keys and my charged cell phone in my pocket, ready to go.

Because if something went down between me and the guy who is about to let me inside his house—like, he tried to jump me for my money or something—how do I know he's alone? How am I gonna know that there wasn't someone else outside, waiting to start up the van and roll it somewhere that no one could see it, so no one would ever know I was there? There was no way I could have known that. So I had to be extra careful on the road alone. You don't take any chances when you're in those situations.

Sure, picking by yourself is great, because you don't have any competition. Sometimes a pick goes better when it's one-on-one and the seller's not distracted. But you can also get more done in less time when there's two of you.

As Mike says, sometimes it can be pretty scary. We like to go to properties that are off the beaten track, out in the country. There's more space there and usually more things to pick. But a lot of the time, it's not the extra acreage that made them choose to live off the main grid: they want to be left alone. Maybe they've got something going on that they don't want the public in on—you never know.

We've had guns in our faces. We've had dogs sicced on us. We've had people threaten to beat us up. And we always keep the fear buried deep in the back of our brains that if we knock on the wrong door, we'll end up being kidnapped and tortured like the guy in the movie *Misery*. It's not *too* far-fetched. (Hmm. Maybe we should pitch a movie about pickers who go down some long dirt road to a house back in the mountains and are never seen again. It'd be a horror movie, for sure.)

All that said, having someone along to have your back is a good idea, at least on longer trips or on picks that are really out of the way. There are some places we've picked on the series that neither of us would have attempted to pick alone. As nice as the Mole Man was, and as cool as his underground house was to pick, neither of us would have ever gone down there alone.

Whether you're picking alone or with another person, you should always let someone else know where you're headed. We have Danielle keeping track of us, but other pickers don't have a built-in tracking device like her.

Think of it like going camping. You wouldn't go out into the woods overnight without telling someone where you'll be, and you shouldn't go on a big pick trip without leaving a trail of crumbs, either. Even if it's vague, like "Today we're going to hit Boulder Pass and Wing Pass, and the next day we're heading down to those little towns close to the Cherokee River," that's enough info to find you if you don't turn up in a few days: if the last time anyone heard from you is in Wing Pass, chances are you're between there and Cherokee

River. That little bit of information narrows down a potential search area tremendously.

Besides being safer, it's just more fun to have company on the road. Picking alone is kind of like fishing by yourself: you catch the big one and have to let it go, and you're the only guy who saw it. We always see things we can't buy that blow our minds, and it's not half as fun to recall it if there was no one with you to see it for themselves.

PICKING TAKES STAMINA

In life and in picking, it's good to remember that your first instinct is usually the right one to follow. Sometimes we physically feel a tug in our stomachs when we walk away from something that has some kind of weird magical pull we're trying to ignore. When we feel that, we know to turn around.

You are learning and have to go through the layers, the process. It is tiring and monotonous. But go with your gut—and go the extra mile. Check out everything that catches your eye, or you'll regret it. There's nothing worse than driving down the road, thinking, "Darn—I should have opened the drawers in that dresser." Because by the time you get the chance to go back, someone else will have done it.

5

SHOP 'TIL YOU POP

HOW TO MAKE DEALS
AND SEAL THEM, TOO

SO, YOU SEE A TOBACCO-CUTTER YOU LIKE—
MAYBE IT HAS A LITTLE BIT OF ADVERTISING
ON IT THAT MAKES IT MORE COLLECTIBLE. SO,
YOU POP ON IT FOR $125. POW! THEN YOU FIND
OUT THEY'RE ONLY WORTH $75. NOW YOU'RE
DOWN $50, AT LEAST. BUT THAT'S PART OF IT.
SOMETIMES YOU TAKE A CHANCE ON SOME-
THING AND YOU GET SCREWED. BUT YOU
NEVER FORGET THOSE MOMENTS—THAT'S
WHAT I CALL PAYING FOR YOUR EDUCATION.

—Mike Wolfe

Picking is an emotional roller-coaster. There are major highs and lows out there on the road. It takes time and patience—picking is a real numbers game. That means chances are, if you make ten stops, you're only gonna score at one of them. Not great odds, but it's all part of the job.

On the road, we constantly see things we think we can't live without, only to be told by the owner that we can't buy them, no matter what price we offer. Pickers have to learn to deal with hearing people say no.

They also have to be willing to *say* no. Good pickers know how to pace themselves—we call it "slowing your roll." Unless your last name is Rockefeller, you can't come into a pick going ninety miles an hour, buying up everything that looks kinda good. We most certainly can't, so we've learned to hold back; otherwise we'll end up blowing our whole budget on the first amazing thing we come across, when the adrenaline is pumping and we're not thinking rationally.

Another reason we have to keep our mind on our money is that we never know what's going to happen every day. We can be out for weeks at a time and come back with next to nothing in our van, or we can make one unplanned stop on some back road we take out of sheer curiosity and find a huge honey hole. Then, boom! We've filled the van so full we can barely see out the back windows.

A picker is only as good as his last pick; no one can say what's coming tomorrow. As stressful as this reality is, it's that constant tension—will we or won't we?—that makes what we do so much fun. You literally never know what's coming next. And even if the road does take you somewhere amazing, you still don't know whether you'll be able to buy anything when you get there.

That's when your ace negotiation skills have to kick in.

POPPING BASICS

We're not out there just buying stuff to be buying things.

If someone tells us they don't want to sell a piece we really, really want to buy, from our perspective that's usually not the end of the story. If we can make the case to our consciences that we're not asking the person to give up something that has a huge emotional value to them, we'll ask them to dance—picker slang for negotiating.

Negotiating is a game, and we're in it to win it. One of the most important things we do when we start talking money is to shut the hell up. Pickers never want to be the first to name a price. Always let the seller do it.

One of Mike's favorite lines to use when we're negotiating is "I can't buy it and sell it"—a phrase he whips out when a seller asks him to be the first in the price-naming game. When a picker is the first to say a number, it can ultimately hurt his ability to get a lower price, which is the number-one priority in our business.

Think about it: a seller asks what you'll give for a kitschy 1970s velvet painting you like. You say $100—a lot more than she thinks it's worth and a higher price than she would have opened with had she been asked to name the price. You could have gotten it for less if you'd gone about the negotiations in a different way. But after you say you're willing to give her $100, it's hard to backpedal and offer her $80. You're pretty much locked into giving up a Benjamin if you want to take the painting home.

VELVET PAINTINGS

Black-velvet paintings were first produced in ancient Kashmir, but hit their height of popularity in the United States when production heated up in Mexico in the 1970s.

Another thing we can assume when someone agrees to a price we've offered too quickly is that we don't know as much about the object as we thought we did. We fully admit that we don't know everything there is to know about antiques and collectibles; we just buy what we like and what we know will sell to our clients. So we always try to turn what could be seen as a loss into a learning experience. We ask the seller to tell us a little about the history of the piece in question and why it's worth what she says it is.

So, while we may walk away from the pick several dollars poorer than we were when we arrived, at least we walk away feeling like the sale wasn't a total loss. That's what we call paying for your education. Get to know it, because it happens a lot in this biz.

OLD POKER FACE

The key to not making mistakes like overpaying is to keep your cool. Pickers have to play Cool Hand Luke when they're working on a site, and especially when they're negotiating.

For example, you don't want to walk into someone's storage shed and go, "Oh my god! I've been looking for that *Planet of the Apes* lunchbox for fifteen years! I have the thermos; if I can buy this, I have the total set!" Bad way to play it. You don't want to show that your heart is pounding out of your chest. You don't want to show that your eyeballs are ready to pop out of your head.

When you geek out on something, the seller knows he's got you,

LUNCH BOXES

The earliest examples of lunch boxes appeared in the mid-1800s and steadily increased in popularity as factory work increased. As more Americans came to work away from home, it became increasingly necessary to transport their lunches. Through the 1950s, most lunch boxes were made of tin or aluminum. The first plastic children's lunch boxes were made in the 1960s, and today most are made of aluminum, vinyl, and foam insulation. Mickey Mouse was the first cartoon character to be featured on a lunch box. That particular piece was produced in 1935 by Geuder, Frey and Paeschke, a Milwaukee-based company.

and he'll probably end up asking for more than they would have before you went all gooey.

Frank is the King of Cool on picks. He keeps calm and never lets on how much he wants something, so the seller can never really be sure what's on his mind:

I'm a thinker. I like to stand back and observe the scene before I express interest in something—and I don't get too excited about anything. Even if I do find something amazing I've been looking for forever, I try to keep a straight face. I don't want to show my cards.

If I see something amazing, I'll just go, "Hey, that thing's kinda neat," and move on. Then I come back to it later, so I don't look overly excited to the seller.

If I'm on the fence about buying something and feel like I need to talk myself into buying it, I'll walk away over $20 if my heart's not in it. Like, I say I'll pay $1,980 for something, but the seller is stuck at $2,000. I'm out. No sale.

But if I'm really into something and want it badly, I'll pay whatever they want. Of course, I'm going to try and get the

best price out of them that I can, but I go into the back-and-
forth knowing that no matter what, I'm gonna pop on it.

REALITY SHOW

Sentimentality can drive the price of things way up. You can forget market prices in situations where people are feeling nostalgic: what someone will pay for the item in a retail situation means nothing to someone who is considering giving up the fiddle their great-great-grandfather played in a bluegrass band back in the day. You can't put a price on a memory.

As we said earlier in the book, we're not in the business of taking people's heirlooms away. We actually sometimes refuse to buy really rare or one-of-a-kind things that we think sellers should hold on to.

And we never get upset at a seller who doesn't want to sell an item that's been in their family for a long time; it's completely understandable to have that kind of sentimental attachment. We tell them that while we'll eventually find someone who will appreciate it, no one will ever appreciate it as much as their family will.

It's a good technique, pointing out how a picker can take something that isn't being used and take it back into the world where someone can enjoy it. But it doesn't work in every situation. Picking heirlooms is pretty touchy, and you have to be able to walk a pretty thin and delicate line. It's easy to piss somebody off or insult them by offering them a valid price on something that they think is priceless.

Another effective way to ease people into selling is to point out flaws in the thing you want to buy. It's like the jointed Steiff teddy bear that we bought from the prop stylist Ruby in Tennessee: it was in terrible condition, and even though collectors don't mind that

STEIFF

The German company was started in 1880 by Margarete Steiff, a seamstress who was confined to a wheelchair after contracting polio as a child. She originally made stuffed elephants to be used as pincushions. When kids started playing with the cushions, she expanded production to other stuffed animals. Her brother and nephew carried on the business, and Steiff continues to make plush toys today. Steiff is known for both high quality and prices reflecting their founder's motto: "Only the Best Is Good Enough for Children."

kind of thing (this is one of those cases when visible age makes something even more valuable—something we'll talk about more later), it gave us some leverage when it came time to talk money with her.

TITLE MATCH

Buying cars and bikes is pretty complicated. You don't just settle on a price and roll the thing out of the garage and ride it off into the sunset. Basically, anything motorized—cars, motorcycles, and scooters are the main ones—has to have a title in order to be driven on the road. So, when you pick something that's motorized, make sure it comes with a title; you probably won't be able to resell it otherwise. (Some states have slightly different variations on title laws, so it's a good idea to check them out before you buy or sell a car or bike, just to avoid any problems down the line.)

A missing title isn't the absolute end of the world. You can get a new one, but it takes lots of time and money. Because of this, lost titles can play a big part in the negotiating process.

Here's Frank's take on making a missing title work in a buyer's favor:

*Let's say a guy wants $800 for his motorcycle; only problem is
he doesn't have the title. It's gonna cost me at least $500 to get
a new one drawn up—not to mention paperwork and hassle—
so I'm going to take that number off the top of the top offer.
Now, what was once an $800 bike is worth only $300.*

*Now, you never know if the seller will go for that—it's a
pretty solid line of reasoning; he may very well laugh in your
face. But it's definitely worth giving this route a shot, especially
if you're planning on using the bike for parts anyway—which
is not necessarily something you want to reveal in negotiations,
but a good thing to remember when you have the chance to
pop on a rare piece that's in bad condition.*

BUYING WITHIN YOUR MEANS

If you take one thing away from this chapter, let it be this: never pay
the first price you're quoted. That's like paying retail.

Half the fun of picking is dickering back and forth with a seller,
trying to come to a price you can agree on. If the seller starts at $75
for an old telescope, you say $50, knowing that you'll be willing to
pay $65 if he gives you a hard time. (It's a good rule of thumb to bid
a lot less than you're actually willing to give—say, $100 if you're will-
ing to pay $150, or $3,000 if you're willing to pay $3,500; that way
you have room to haggle.)

You can't walk into a new pick thinking like a gambler, throw-
ing down five Gs on something you don't know anything about,
hoping to maybe squeeze $6,000 or $7,000 out of it when you sell it
at retail. Confidence can only get you so far in picking. Bad business is bad business, no matter how cocky you act.

When we're out on the road, we have to be very careful about
what we spend our money on. We have to be sure that we can at
least double our money on most things in order to cover our travel

TELESCOPES

Very old telescopes are rare today, because the glass optic and tubes are so fragile. Most have broken or were badly dented over the years. Brass telescopes are the most common, and often had leather or wood covering that might include the maker's name etched on the side.

expenses, pay Danielle and the rest of the overhead at Antique Archaeology, and be able to bank a little at the end. Plus, remember that pickers don't score at every stop. You can go on twenty-five picks and only walk away with two or three things worth your time. Quantity does not equal quality in the world of picking.

Every pick depends on the timing and atmosphere, including the seller's mood and the time and energy everyone had to devote to the effort. From the outside, a prospective site might appear to be the biggest mega-pick ever, but a picker still might walk away empty-handed if the seller's not in the mood or gets his nose out of joint.

Pricing is always a mixed bag. Sometimes a picker can get away with a steal, while other times they pay way too much. Getting the best deal often depends on a picker's experience and ability to bargain.

Frank has become kind of famous for the deals he makes when he bundles. This involves gathering up several different items while you're touring a property, putting them in one pile and making one all-inclusive offer on the bunch. If the seller asks for more than you're willing to pay, you can remove pieces, one by one, until you find a number you can agree on.

Bundling works especially well with smalls. Bundling is a good way to buy the contents of boxes full of random things; as long as there's one piece in there that will make you money, the rest is icing.

BE PREPARED

Probably more than 90 percent of our sales are made on the spot. That's why you've got to go in with your big guns loaded. As Frank likes to say, never take a knife to a gunfight. Always have money in your pocket. There have been times when we've had $100 or $500 in cash on us and a seller says, okay, I'll take $1,000 for that old Yamaha racer.

So you tell him you'll give him $500 today and drop the rest off tomorrow. This scenario might play out several different ways. One less-than-desirable outcome has the seller refusing to sell the bike until you bring him the whole $1,000. You tell the guy you'll bring the entire amount to him tomorrow; he seems cool with it. But then, when you turn up the next day, cash in hand, the bike is gone. He's convinced another dude to give him more money, using your offer as a backup. If you'd just had the $1,000 in your pocket, the deal would have been done.

The moral of that story is: the time to buy something is when it's in front of you. Not tomorrow. Not next week. Now.

Maybe you don't have room in your car. Or maybe your bank account's not very flush at the moment. No excuses. Call a friend to come meet you in a bigger car or make a plan to eat ramen noodles for a week so you can afford the thing. But don't leave it. The Laws of Picking dictate that it won't be there when you come back.

TRANSPORTING YOUR PICKS

Most folks don't have a cargo van. But even if you're picking out of a Honda coupe, there are still things to keep in the trunk that will make transporting your treasures easier, including newspapers, rags, and empty boxes in several different widths and heights.

PICKING 101

Or the item may still be there but the seller may have promised it to someone else, using your last bid as ammo. Or he will have just flat-out changed his mind.

This happened to Frank a few years ago, when he was trying to pop on a Triumph motorcycle. He and the guy dickered back and forth—as you do—stuck on the $100 difference between the guy's asking price of $600 and Frank's final offer of $500. So, Frank gets in his car and leaves.

Twenty miles down the road, he has one of those "uh-oh" moments; he could feel in his gut that he'd passed up something really good. So he turned around and headed back to the seller's farm.

When he got there, the price of the bike had changed: the bike was now $800. Was that switcheroo out of spite? That was probably some of it. But the main reason he jacked the price up was that Frank coming back assured him that he was serious about buying. And he was: Frank ended up laying down $800. Yet another example of paying for your education.

SHOW THEM THE MONEY

There is no magic amount of cash that a picker needs to carry on a pick. It changes from person to person, depending on what they're looking for, how much they want to buy, and what their budget is. The amount can also reflect how long you're going to be out on your pick.

It really depends on what you buy. Of course, if you're picking a $20,000 crystal chandelier, you're probably not going to whip that out of your wallet. That kind of pick requires you to pay with a check or money order.

Otherwise, having a few thousand dollars broken down into different denominations is smart—especially when you're making change after an intense negotiation. You'll blow your cover if you pull out $100 after swearing up and down that you're down to your last $60.

For the most part, we endorse the "pay as you go" way of doing business. Saying to someone you're going to give them $1,000 and actually putting it in their hand are two totally different things.

Once you get some money out in the open—and once they feel how good a stack of hundreds feels in their hands—it loosens them up a little bit. It also lets them know you're serious. Five minutes before the first sale, they might have been, like, "No, I think I'm going to keep this piece of art pottery. I don't want to sell it quite yet: it looks cute in my kitchen window." And then, once they see that green, they change their mind—they suddenly remember that they need to put new carpet down in their den or get new teeth or something. Then it becomes, "Well, you know, maybe I can sell it after all. I can put another vase in that spot . . ."

What really seals the deal is when you do what we suggested before and bring it to their attention that the thing you want to buy is just sitting around in a dark room, not being enjoyed by anyone. Once they start thinking about that point, the choice between getting $1,000 in cash on the spot and keeping a broken slot machine they've had holed up in their attic for forty years gets pretty easy.

If we're interested in something that a seller has an emotional attachment to, and she tells us she wants to think about it overnight before letting us pop, we make sure to give her a solid number to mull

SLOT MACHINES

These lever-operated gambling machines were first introduced in the late 1880s by Charles Fey in San Francisco. Some of the machines' more colorful nicknames include "one-armed bandit" and "fruit machine," due to the apples, oranges, and other edibles pictured on the spinning reels.

over. Then, that night, instead of thinking about the thing they're getting rid of, they'll be thinking about the cash. When they have a number, it will never leave their mind, whether they're in the shower, doing dishes, pulling on their pants, mowing the yard—it becomes all about the price.

Once they say they'll sell, put the money in their hands as soon as you can. That makes it a lot harder for them to back out, which does happen sometimes. If you get the cash flowing early in the pick, while you're still building a rapport with the seller, you're probably gonna get a better price on the things you buy after that.

LOAD 'EM UP

When we're on the road, we have to be conscious of what we're buying. If we're any more than a half a day's drive away from the store, we have to edit our picks pretty closely. This isn't a bad thing: we love big things but they don't sell as quickly as smalls. So, having a limited amount of space keeps us lean and mean and helps us avoid overbuying.

Our picks are always cash-and-carry—with us doing both the giving out of the cash and the carrying out of the stash. We never assume that the price we offer will include help with labor; we usually have to negotiate that in—offer $20 more for some extra muscle. However, most of the folks we deal with offer to help us if they're physically able.

Sometimes, though, we're on our own and we have to make it work. Mike has been known to use old screen doors as rickshaws to pull heavy things across big properties; that's how he was able to rescue some high-dollar Harley parts that were buried way back in some junkyard a few years ago.

There have been times when we've picked things that even two people can't move. A few years ago, we found an oversize two-sided porcelain-and-neon sign at a drugstore that had gone out of business. The man who sold it to us couldn't help load it up. So, we went across the street and offered $20 to a big guy having lunch at a Burger King to help us load up the sign once he'd finished his Whopper.

6
WHAT'S IT WORTH?
HOW TO PRICE AND CARE FOR YOUR FINDS

WE'RE BOTH PRETTY KNOWLEDGEABLE BUT DON'T KNOW EVERYTHING THERE IS TO KNOW ABOUT EVERY PIECE WE BUY. THAT'S WHY WE RELY ON EXPERTS IN DIFFERENT FIELDS TO HELP US PUT VALUES ON CERTAIN ITEMS. LIKE OUR GUY BILL. HE'S AMAZING. HE KNOWS EVERYTHING ABOUT TOYS. HE'S GONNA HELP US PUT A VALUE ON THIS ITEM SO WE FEEL COMFORTABLE SELLING IT.

—Mike Wolfe

When we're out picking, we're not looking for things that you find in every antique shop from here to Timbuktu; we're not in this to fill the van up with big pieces of Eastlake furniture and bad reproduction paintings. We want things that are unusual, that are interesting, that are different. We want things that are thought-provoking, weird even.

The dealers and collectors we sell to are pretty knowledgeable; they've been doing this a long time and they've seen thousands of pieces and a lot of trends come and go. We want to surprise them and give them something they haven't seen before. And, a lot of the time, these things aren't necessarily expensive or even in the best shape. (If we had a nickel for every time someone told us, "I thought you'd want to buy the antiques and all you guys wanted to buy was the crap," we might never have to pick again.) What they do have is soul.

A picker has to have a good eye. Having "an eye" is like having good taste: either you have it or you don't. And that brings us to the concept of "good junk" and "bad junk"—yes, there is a difference. But it's a very fine line, especially when you take into account how subjective this whole business is—you know, the old "one man's trash is another man's treasure" thing. The cool old beat-up stuff that we think is amazing is total scrap to another picker.

The key to rocking it as a picker isn't to buy things that are worth the most money: it's figuring out what you like to pick and making that your focus. Yes, making money is great and necessary for us to do what we do, but it's not what keeps us on the road.

We all have to buy things we don't give a darn about, from time to time, but that's usually just to make ends meet until we can go back out in search of things we really want to buy. But we can make a living digging ditches and not work half as hard (or get half as dirty) as we do on a pick. We're in this for the thrill of the hunt.

As we're sure you've figured out by now, this book isn't a price guide. We can't start to tell you how to put an exact number on all the stuff you're going to come across on your picks; we'd have to put out a hundred-volume book set if we wanted to even scratch the surface in that area. But there are some pointers we can share when it comes to pickers getting themselves ready to go out, and value-related things that they can keep in mind when they're hitting the gravel for a major free-style spree.

SERVING IT UP FARM-FRESH

We've always liked stuff that looks as though it just rolled out of a barn; that's what we call "farm-fresh." When we first started out as pickers, neither of us had the knowledge or money to restore things; we'd just clean them up the best we could with what we had. Over the years, we figured out that that's the look we like: we'd rather have things that look lived-in—you know, kind of worn and a little decrepit—than something that looks brand-new.

We find that most people we deal with connect more with the roached-out Esso gas signage we buy than they do with the perfect reproductions they see at the local antique mall. We think it's because they associate age and wear with memories—like, they know that the thing they're buying had a full life before they came into the picture. They can see the history in the rust, and they connect emotionally to the piece that way. Now, if we'd blasted it with water or cleaning fluid, taking all the age away, it would look like any other sign hanging in an antique mall. And in our opinion—one that not everyone shares, by the way—that's boring.

Believe it or not, you don't always need to clean up your picks before you try to sell them. Some collectors would rather have the original wear and tear of an item visible, to add authenticity or a rustic edge.

For that reason, people in the antiques industry aren't restoring things very much anymore. The going look right now in the design market is what they call the "heritage" movement, which means lots of simple, American-made things that look like they have a history, the longer the better. Natural wear and tear is almost a badge of honor.

Another problem with trying to "improve" something that's naturally aged or rusted is that once you start cleaning, you sometimes don't know when to stop.

Let's say you're dealing with a boy's bike from the 1930s. It's been inside a damp garage for the last fifty years, and looks it. You start small—you just want to clean a little bit of the rust off the handlebars. But then they start to look so good that the rest of the bike looks weird. One thing leads to another, and voilà! The bike looks brand-new. Not good.

There is such a thing as over-restoring—and you don't want to go there. If you make something look too new, it loses its original vibe. Also, if something is too clean and neat, you stop looking at

REPAIRS

Typically, whenever you add something to an antique, it automatically depreciates the value, so you want to be careful about what you do and whom you trust to do it. Do your homework before having something repaired; ask experts in your area whom they'd recommend to do the job and then quiz them thoroughly before allowing them to do any work.

PICKING 101

the piece; all you can see is the quality of the restoration. It's, like, "Wow, I've never seen a bike that old so shiny!" And you won't ever again—unless it gets the same kind of makeover.

Then again, while we're hesitant to restore the look of all the roached-out things we find on picks, we usually don't mind repairing them if it means more money for us on the back end.

You have to be careful, though. Do your homework before having something repaired; ask experts in your area whom they'd recommend to do the job.

Here's Frank's take on it:

> *If I find a motorcycle in a million pieces, I'll assemble it to give someone more of an idea of what they're buying. Or if a part is rotting or missing on a piece of furniture, we'll take care of that kind of thing.*
>
> *I just bought a toy that a horse had stepped on. I have a guy who works on toys for me, and I took it to him. He didn't touch it restoration-wise, but he straightened it out. He bent it back into the original shape and soldered it in a few places. I was still able to sell it; you just have to be honest with the person you're selling it to. You can't tell them it's in the original condition if it's been fixed.*

Something else to remember on the restoration/repair note: make sure to take before-and-after pictures that show any changes that were made. When you tell a buyer you had something fixed up, a lot of the time they'll ask to see these shots.

PUTTING IT IN REVERSE

For at least ten years, the big thing for furniture manufacturers has been to take new reproductions and age them so they'll look freshly picked. People actually want their things to look old—and they're paying a lot of money for it.

Of course, we're all about bringing it to them farm-fresh; reproduction isn't our thing. But the process is interesting and something good to know about.

You think of furniture guys as working in a shop with wood curls on the floor and toolboxes full of hammers and saws. But the guys who specialize in aging things work in offices that look like science labs. There are bottles of concoctions sitting everywhere that they combine to give certain effects. They use herbicides and pesticides to rust things in an artful way and chemicals like gun bluing agents to add years. Each potion, used in different combinations or left on for certain amounts of time, gives a different kind of effect. Some people don't want the rust to be orange; they want it to be brown. These guys can make that happen. Let's say you want a porcelain sign to look like it had been in a shallow ditch outside a barn in rural Pennsylvania for fifty years. They can do that, too.

The same type of thing is happening in the denim industry. The majority of mainstream jeans buyers want their pants to look like they were worn by chain-gang members—or hard-partying rock stars, take your pick: both of those guys push their clothes to the limit. So, denim specialists have come up with ways to get the ripped-slashed-and-worn-all-over look by beating them up with rocks, slashing them with razor blades, and splashing them with bleach to get the right effect.

Whether you're talking blue jeans or old farm equipment signs, old is now what's new.

BUYING WHAT'S HOT

A picker's taste is his signature. In this business, the way you differentiate yourself from Jersey John and every other picker working the country right now is by the things you buy and sell. But the reality is that not everyone has your taste and interests. For example, not every client we have is going to want to buy old motorcycles and antique metal toys, two categories that we both love to look for. So, we try to be practical and find items that we know we can move quickly, in addition to the stuff that feeds our souls.

In order to find out what's going to be a lucrative pick, we turn to the world of interiors for clues, whether that's at stores, in magazines or books, or by talking to experts in the field about big trends to look for and what's selling in design stores.

Believe it or not, when we're not picking, we like to go shopping; we spend a lot of time on the road scouting specialty stores and boutiques that deal in vintage interiors. This is one of the ways that we get inspired and get ideas for what to pick. (We love to sell to interior stores, so we also use this time to get new clients; more on that in the next chapter.)

When we come across a store we like, we take careful mental notes. We check out the colors they use to decorate, how the space is laid out, how they display things, what they're selling, and—this is key—what they're not selling. All these things help us figure out what's worth buying when we're out in the field.

For example, let's say we come across a great pair of Victorian wrought-iron light fixtures in a barn in Wisconsin. It's a lot easier to make a decision on whether to pop or not if you know that they'd fit in with the décor at your favorite interior shop. Once you see how something is being used by the pros, you can buy it with a clear conscience: you know it's popular and you know you can sell it later.

If hanging out in design stores isn't your thing, don't worry. You don't have to go shopping to know what's selling. Magazines like *Martha Stewart Living, House Beautiful*, and *Country Living* do it for you. Flipping through an interiors publication or checking out popular design blogs is a great way to find out what's in. You don't

WROUGHT IRON

Iron has been used for weapons and jewelry as early as 3000 BC. Wrought iron is an iron alloy with a low carbon content that gives it a visible "wood grain." It was used in architecture and furniture design for hundreds of years before the low cost of steel made its use all but obsolete in the 1960s. Use of wrought iron reached its peak in the 1860s for use in railways and warships. The Eiffel Tower, completed in 1889, is one of the most famous wrought-iron structures.

even have to spend a lot of time reading the fine print under the pictures; just looking at the pictures is enough to get the idea of how things are being used.

The mainstream media really helps drive the collectibles market. The ideas may come from the smaller stores and the interior designers and decorators who shop there, but once that's established, then big companies follow the lead.

Here's an example. A few years ago, Mike was talking to a designer who told him that she was using a lot of old brass blade fans in her work. That put his antenna up; he started seeking them out and sold them like crazy to his decorator clients. Sure enough, less than a year later, brass blade fans were suddenly being sold at home stores all over the country.

Retail stores and magazines aren't the only places to look when you want to get inspired. You can do the same thing at antique malls and fairs. One of the best ways to learn about what's in style—not to mention expand your knowledge base—is to spend the afternoon at a flea market walking up and down the aisles, checking out the stock and talking to dealers who carry things you're interested in.

At antique malls, talk to the folks behind the front desk and see what they say is moving. Find out what the most popular booths in the mall are and check them out, not only to see what they have but how it's displayed, too. The idea is to keep your eyes—and your mind—open to new ideas.

Here's Mike's flea market MO:

Pickers are naturally kind of standoffish. Most of them don't want to give away any of their knowledge, because they don't want more competition. Personally, I've never really cared about that. I've always been very secure and content with my own abilities, so it's, like, Copy me! Please! I don't care. You're not me! We're all different when it comes to the things we pick.

If I go to the flea market and pass a table with more than a few things that I think are cool, I'll stop and give it a closer look. A guy like that, I want to know what makes him tick. I want to figure out his signature.

Because that's what a designer's store or a dealer's flea market booth is: it's his creation. The picker renting this space is an artist and this booth is his palette. And the things he's picked are what he uses to paint. And if I can appreciate what he's created, I'll stop and ask questions about things he has that I'm not familiar with. I try to use pickers whose taste I admire, to educate myself. We all kind of work together that way.

When you find a dealer whose taste you dig, introduce yourself. What do you have to lose? Ask the guy to show you some of his favorite things. Maybe he'll teach you something, maybe he's full of crap—who knows. The answer is you don't, unless you ask.

If he is a collector, you're in luck. Collectors usually love to talk about their stuff and show off what they know. When we run into someone who knows a whole lot about one thing, we try to pick his brain as much as we can. We take these meetings as opportunities to learn about areas of the antiques-and-collectibles business that are foreign to us.

Make sure to pick up as many things as you can, too. Some vendors are weird about it, so if the piece is really fragile or behind glass, ask before you reach out and touch it. But being familiar with the heft of a piece can come in quite handy down the line, when, say, you're trying to authenticate a cast-iron bank by its weight. (Hint: old cast iron that was used to make early banks was much heavier than the stuff they use in repop. Also: older versions have a mushroom-y smell that newer cast-iron pieces don't have.)

BEWARE THE REPOP

There are only a few things that strike true fear in the heart of a picker. Rabid dogs not on leashes are one; running out of gas on the long, sad road between Nowheresville and Crazytown is another. But even more than those terrible things, we fear the repop.

Reproductions of antiques make our job harder than it already is. It's difficult enough trying to figure out whether something you want to pop on can be resold, but adding the presence of antique impostors makes things even tougher.

There are all types of reproductions out there in the collectibles market. From huge pieces of furniture to tiny things like marbles and coins, copies have been floating around in the world of antiques before anyone ever thought to call it a business.

Why is repop so popular? A few reasons. First off, sales of copies are geared toward people who want to own expensive things but can't afford to buy them. Repop pieces often use inferior materials and craftsmanship; scrimping on manufacturing passes the savings along to the buyer.

Repop also comes into play when the demand for a certain antique collectible is greater than the numbers that were originally made. To use the brass blade fan example again, once every decorator caught on to that trend, all the mass-market stores wanted to reproduce them

MARBLES

Many different kinds of marbles were used in games in ancient Egypt, Rome, and India. The first mass-produced ceramic marbles were made in the 1870s in Germany. The collectible ones we see today are mostly from 1890 or later. In 1903, the first mass-produced glass marbles were made in the United States. Game rules, objects, and customs vary widely across cultures. Today, over twelve million marbles are produced every day.

COINS

The origin of the first coins is uncertain, but historians do know that the ancient Greeks began minting and using coins in 700 BC. The Greeks then spread coins and currency to the rest of the Mediterranean and Middle Eastern region. The most valuable collectible coins are those that circulated for the shortest time or were printed with a mistake. Coins with historical relevance, such as those issued at a coronation or death of a public figure, are also particularly valuable.

and cash in, since they know that there's no way everyone who wants an antique fan can find one in good shape.

Repop producers push the idea that instead of trying to own one of the very rare real things, why not buy a copy that looks exactly the same? From a sales standpoint, it makes total sense. But for people that pride themselves on buying based on the authenticity of an item, it confuses things. A lot of high-end copiers are really on their game and it can be hard to tell the old from the new.

Sometimes ID'ing repop is as easy as finding the "Made in China" sticker on the bottom of a painted metal toy you see on the shelves of a big chain store. Other times, it's not spelled out for you like that. Since repop has been popular for a long time, sometimes there is more than just one copy of an original floating around; manufacturers might have made more than one production run over many decades. That means that not only do you have to tell the original 1920s toy from the brand-new repop but you have to deal with the 1958 run and the reissue in 1976. Bottom line, multiple runs mean there's even more impostors to look out for.

One thing to remember is that you rarely find a really faithful reproduction of intricate mechanical items. Repop-makers don't want to spend a lot of money, so they cut lots of corners and use new materials when they can. A picker with any kind of experience knows a repop clock or radio when he sees one: the piece may look amazing and true to the original on the outside, but the inside will be full of new components. That is a dead giveaway.

Size is another thing repop makers like to change. Let's say the original model of the antique desk clock they're copying was ten inches tall; the "antique" repop might measure up at ten-and-a-half inches. Close, but no cigar—and, we hope for the picker who was thinking about popping on it, no sale.

But really the only way to be 100 percent sure that the painted miniature tin car from the 30s you want to buy isn't a reproduction is to know a hell of a lot about painted tin car toys from the 30s.

If you don't have all that knowledge, then just go with your gut: most of the time, if you think it's a reproduction, it is. If something looks great for its age and is priced for a steal, it doesn't just seem like the deal is too good to be true, it probably is. Walk on by.

Otherwise, that's why we keep our expert friends close at hand.

GENUINE AUTHENTIC

People like to collect things with pedigree—well, at least some people do. Frank, personally, thinks it's kind of silly:

As a general rule, I've found that motorcycles that belonged to famous people run as well or as badly as those that were driven by regular people. Really, does anyone think that if Billy Idol used to own the bike they're buying, it's any more special than one owned by Joe Blow?

Most people we deal with don't care one way or the other, but there are some collectors out there who would rather buy items that can be authenticated. So, if you can prove to them that, you know, Elvis wore the ring you're selling in the movie Blue Hawaii, *and you have pictures as proof and a note from the jeweler who sold it to him, saying the ring is legit, then you're going to be more likely to make a sale to someone who's a big fan and really wants something that the King wore.*

Another thing that makes a piece seem more special in some people's eyes is if it ever was directly featured in a newspaper or magazine story. Let's say you're selling a metal floor lamp from the late 60s that was owned by Paul Newman; if you can find a picture of the room where he used the lamp in the back issue of *Architec-*

THINGS THAT ADD VALUE

These can elevate an iffy piece to must-have status.

Good condition: Self-explanatory. Look for pieces with no chips, tears, or rips, that don't have missing parts.

Rarity: Knowing how many individual items or runs a collectible has had can help you determine how much it's worth.

Paperwork: Written authentication is a plus in some collectors' books, especially when you're talking about paintings by notable artists, jewelry, and motorized things like cars (always look for brochures and manuals).

Original packaging: Extra points if it's never been opened.

A good story: People love to buy something that has a history; it brings it to life.

tural Digest, that not only offers more solid proof that you really are selling the real thing but it also makes the lamp look a lot more glamorous in some people's eyes. Make sure to show them the clipping when you're trying to seal the deal.

People buying items that were produced in limited editions or in limited runs like to ask for paper authentication pretty often, too. If you want to get the most money out of a print, check to see if it's numbered; usually, you find this in the lower right-hand corner of the print: the number of prints that were produced is on the bottom, and the number of the print you have in your possession is on top. If you see 33/190, that means you have the 33rd print made out of a run of 190. Prints with smaller runs are the most desirable, because fewer were produced.

EXPERT HELP

In our business, we rely on experts in different fields to help us put value on certain items. So, instead of asking about how to determine the value of a specific item, we've asked some of the antiques and collectibles pros who have been on the series to tell us how they accumulated their knowledge and to suggest how novice pickers can go about educating themselves before they hit the road.

Richard

Richard has been in the antique firearms industry for forty years; he owned his own auction company. Right now he's a consultant for Rock Island Auction Company in the Illinois Quad Cities, which is right across the river from our picker HQ in Le Claire.

We've known Richard for a long time, and he's the go-to guy for firearms for us (and, if we're being honest, pretty much every serious gun aficionado in the world who wants to get the straight 411 on the history and value of their collection). You may remember

Richard from the episode of *American Pickers* where he gave us an appraisal on the Japanese sword our buddy Leland picked up when he was stationed overseas in WWII, but he knows a lot about a huge range of other collectibles as well.

From where Richard stands, as long as a collector knows his subject and takes the process of examining what he's buying from a practical point of view, he'll be fine:

> *Everything is so fast-paced in the collecting world these days. Buyers rely on the Internet and on other people to lay the information about what they're buying in their lap. You can't let this happen: you have to do your own homework.*
>
> *If you're collecting something, learn all you can about it before you buy anything. If there's a book on the subject, get on it.*
>
> *When you get to the stage where you're buying items and starting to determine quality and worth, remember to step back and think about what you're looking at from a practical point of view.*
>
> *Original items—meaning older things that are not reproductions—develop what is called a patina, which is the name for natural aging. Think about how the outside of an old painted wooden barn that's been exposed to the weather for years and years looks; that's patina. And that look is really desirable right now.*
>
> *A lot of people make a mistake and clean up their finds— and I'm not talking about wiping the dust off of something. That's okay. But if a guy has an old cast-iron bank with paint that's naturally chipping off and he takes a wire wheel to it to clean off the loose flakes, he's just ruined it. That bank just lost about 90 percent of its value.*
>
> *I see the same thing happen with old duck decoys. Collectors want them to look like they've been used, like they've been*

floating in water. But sellers sometimes mess up and take them to artists to get them repainted, or clean them up with linseed oil. And that can ruin their value.

There are a few ways to tell if the patina is natural, and they're actually pretty obvious. They all have to do with identifying how the item was originally used and for what purpose.

If there are scratches that have been painted over, that usually means the piece has been cleaned up. If the item were in its original condition, the scratches would go through the paint.

If a seller tells you that the car you're looking at is being sold with the original paint job and the car has thirty thousand miles on it, you should be able to see some road wear. There should be rock chips on the bottom near the wheels.

This is all really common sense. Again, you have to think about how things were originally used and how that might cause them to wear over time.

For example, if you're looking at a toy, it will most likely have some natural dents and scratches from being dropped when a kid was playing with it. Old coins will probably have some nicks on them, the kind that all coins get from being carried together in your pocket.

Just remember: caveat emptor—buyer beware. You have to do your homework; nobody is going to do it for you. A lot of people work off impulse and they end up regretting it. Very seldom does blind luck get you a good deal.

Zeff

Zeff owns a really cool antique store called Heritage Antiques in Lexington, Kentucky. He's got a broad knowledge about a variety of things, from fine art and bronzes to good, solid American furniture, which is really plentiful in that part of the country (horses = rich people).

But Zeff says that in his job, he's weighed in with his opinion on the value of things, so spectacular they make you fall on the floor to modern Barbie-doll stuff.

When it comes to researching the history of the things that come through his shop, he has some pretty cool tricks up his sleeve:

We weren't wealthy when I was growing up, and from a pretty young age I found out that if I was going to have any money to spend, I'd have to make it myself. My dad ran a flea market in Lexington and tells the story about the first time he set me loose in the parking lot where the dealers set up. I started out with a pocketknife in my pocket, and at the end of the day, I had traded five or six times and had a better pocketknife, $12, and a gold coin. That's how I got started in it.

If someone brings me something I'm not sure about, I've learned to say right up front that I'm happy to give my opinion on it but that it's not something I'm very knowledgeable about, so you really need to see an expert. I've got a really broad knowledge—there's a lot of stuff I have a feeling for, but a lot of things I don't have the slightest idea about. I'm always quick to say that up front.

If it's an Oriental piece—Japanese and Chinese—I have learned to be really careful. There's a lot of it in this region, and it's a huge business. There are Oriental vases that bring in millions of dollars—I don't have them in my store, but I keep up with what's selling in other places. It's the biggest-booming market I've ever witnessed in my history of antiques.

I have a neat trick. I eat at a local place, a high-end Japanese restaurant, pretty regularly and I've gotten to know the people there well. So, when I go, I sometimes take a print with a Japanese signature on it that I'm not sure about and get them to translate it for me. You pay $50 for a great dinner and you get a translation, too—it's an awesome deal.

One thing I found out this way was that there's old Japanese and then there's what kids write today. If you ask anyone younger than forty to translate the writing on an old antique, they can't do it. They'll say, go ask the older guys in the kitchen.

George

Whenever we buy some whacked-out stuff, or stuff we really don't know much about, we call George. He's the pro we turn to when we want to know the history of anything scientific or mechanical: he specializes in STM—science, technology, and mechanical, which includes everything from microscopes to typewriters to steam engines. (He even appraised a piece of the ENIAC, the world's first computer.)

He's based in Chicago now, but has spent a lot of his career in England and on the East Coast, where he worked for big-time auction houses like Christie's and Sotheby's. He clued us in to the value of a steam popcorn popper we picked on the series.

His picking approach is pretty old-school:

You can't just go out picking if you don't know anything. You should have either a very specialized knowledge or a very broad knowledge. You have to know a lot about a little or a little about a lot.

Because I have a pretty specific knowledge, I can see really rare things that go unnoticed by other people. I can go to an auction and watch people spend major money for utter junk while I can buy something for nothing because no one else knows what it is. People collect what they've seen and what other people have seen, and if it's not known, everybody stands away from it: they don't want to be the first to say what it's worth. So, some of the most rare pieces can go for nothing.

I will buy a box lot for $100 because I see something in it that I can sell for $1,500; the rest of the stuff is maybe worth $100 total. But someone else might have bought the same box

*and never known there was anything valuable in it and would
have maybe made back his money plus $50. That happens in
this world all the time.*

*People who want to build their eye can do three main
things: listen, read, and touch. Seek out other people who know
about the things you want to know more about and listen to
what they have to say. Collectors love to share; they want to talk
to other collectors. And some of them want to teach the next
generation—they want to make sure there are people to buy their
collections when they die, so the interest in their expertise
doesn't go with them.*

*Read as much as you can about the things you want to
collect, via the Internet and the library. And then go out of
your way to touch as many items as you can—you have to
handle things to really get to know them. Go to auctions, go to
antique shows, go to antique stores and malls and hold things
you want to learn more about. You've got to know the stuff
intimately before you can buy it with any sort of confidence.*

*And, finally, don't buy a darn thing for a long time, or don't
spend a lot of money when you do. You're going to mess up.
That's how you learn.*

Jerry

Jerry has worked as a licensed auctioneer in South Carolina since
1971. He says it's always been his dream to open a museum, and
he's well on his way: he's been collecting for the past forty years.

Jerry thinks that the main thing a picker can do to improve his
track record is to see as many different antiques as you can:

*I started collecting when I was in high school. When I was
seventeen, I'd leave football practice to go picking. The rest of
the boys were going on about women and I was interested in
antiques.*

Antiques have been the one true love of my life. Most of my truly great finds I've stumbled upon; they're not necessarily things I've sought out. Sometimes someone calls you to come look at something they have that you might want; when you get there, something else will catch your eye. You don't care anymore about the thing you came to see.

Back when I started, you had to work with the seat of your britches—you had to know what you were doing on your own. Now everybody is able to look up whatever they need on the Internet. It's an excellent place for gaining knowledge about things you see somewhere else and want to learn more about.

You have to be a collector for a while to learn what's out there before you can start to sell. That's the only way you'll get to know what something's worth. And, you know, you can collect anything. You can collect eggbeaters. And there's an awful lot of eggbeaters out there that cost thousands of dollars—for an eggbeater!

I collect handheld corn shellers, and the really rare ones can go for $4,000 or $5,000. The only way you know the difference between those and the run-of-the-mill shellers is experience. You'll only know what's what after seeing a lot of corn shellers.

Ken

Ken is based near us in Davenport, and he knows a heck of a lot about a lot of things. But anything coin-operated, like jukeboxes and slot machines, and oil and gas memorabilia are his main focus.

Ken knows the deal on cool old signage and advertising in and out and back again, so he's our go-to guy for that kind of stuff, too. Even though we're big fans of buying rusty, holey signs with more than a little wear and tear, we know that not everyone wants the roached-out look we love. So we have total respect for Ken's rule for collecting only the best.

The Internet gives young people starting out in this business so much knowledge that took me thirty years to get. You can find out with a click what something is bringing in the market.

Instead of traveling all over to see what things are going for in different areas, you can go on eBay and just push in what you want and get your answer. The important thing to remember is that you want to look for what the item sells for, not what some guy is asking for it. It's important not to get those mixed up.

Also, if you're trying to compare something you have to an identical piece on eBay, remember that you can only compare apples to apples. Make sure that the item you're looking at is in exactly the same condition, or the price won't be accurate.

I'm the kind of guy that doesn't think something can be in too good a condition. A lot of guys think just because a sign is out of the 30s and all beat up and chipped up, it's still worth a lot of money because of when it was made. That's just not true.

Let's say someone who collects Coca-Cola advertising comes across a metal Coke sign that's all beat to hell—like, it's scratched up and has a bullet hole through it. And the guy thinks, "That's okay; it gives it character." Well, it's junk to me. I don't buy that kind of stuff. There are people who say, "Hey, this sign is a little beat up, so I'm only asking $200 for it." That won't fly for the kind of guys I deal with: they want a sign

COCA-COLA

John S. Pemberton introduced Coca-Cola in 1886, and, with it, a new way of advertising. His willingness to put the Coca-Cola logo and accompanying slogans on everything from clocks to calendars essentially created a whole new division of collectibles.

that's perfect, and they'll pay $1,200 to get it. Perfect is always gonna be perfect; its value is always gonna be good. You can never be sure of that with things that are damaged.

Sometimes I buy big collections that have a few signs in perfect condition and a lot of rough ones. I keep the nice signs or sell them to collectors for a lot of money. And then I take the rough ones and sell them at the flea market. I try to unload them as quick as I can and hope I can make a little money doing it. Because it's real easy to sell the good stuff, but it's real tough to sell the bad.

Dave

When Mike first started to get into bikes twenty-five years ago, Dave was the guy he went to for advice. Since then, he's pretty much been Mike's mentor when it comes to how you go about learning all there is to know about things that ride on two wheels, though he's a pro at cars, too.

Dave is based in Clinton, Iowa, where he spends most of his time restoring old Harleys. (Get this: a few years ago, he restored the Harley chopper that was used in *Easy Rider.*) He buys, too: as the curator of the National Motorcycle Museum, he's in charge of finding cool old bikes to add to the museum's collection. Not a bad gig.

As you might expect, along the way he's come up with some great tips for gaining knowledge about collecting antique motorcycles. He's a big proponent of using the other collectors and professionals you meet at official collectors' events as a sounding board— something we think is a great idea for any type of collector:

I worked at a chopper shop in the Quad Cities back in the 70s and met a guy named Bob Skeffington, who owned this place called Skeff Cycles. He had an old Indian Chief and I remember thinking that was the most beautiful bike I'd ever seen. I didn't know much about motorcycles back then, but I knew it had to be rare.

Skeff is the guy who really introduced me to the world of motorcycles. He belonged to the Antique Motorcycle Club of America and took me with him to one of their meets in 1977; I haven't missed one since. And now I go to them all over the country.

The Antique Motorcycle Club isn't just any club; it's the club for motorcycle collectors. If you really want to learn about motorcycles by joining an organization of other collectors, this is the one to join. It doesn't cost that much and you get a lot out of it.

Back when I joined the Antique Motorcycle Club, it was a pretty small group; my club number is 200, and now there are thousands and thousands of people involved in it. They sponsor meets and road runs all over the country, so there are a lot of chances to get to know other collectors. I always thought this was great, because you were able to learn a lot directly from the old guys, who always had the best stuff and knew so much about collecting bikes; they were the ones that the younger collectors really looked up to.

Club events are nice, because they bring so many collectors together in one place; you can really bounce ideas off one another. There's a lot of conflicting information out there when it comes to what to buy, and you don't want to have to learn the hard way; you don't want to get ripped off buying replicas. Reproductions are everywhere, and because people now know how to take a new bike and antique it down to where it looks old, there is a lot of room for mistakes, especially since some people aren't afraid to misrepresent them. There's no way to know what's real and what's fake unless you have the right knowledge.

CHANGE OR DIE

A career picker's goal is to be able to continue to make a living buying and selling. In order to do that, you have to stay on your toes, roll with the changes in the market, and never stop expanding your repertoire. There are always new collectors to appeal to, and you should always be trying to figure out how to reach them.

Certain death to a picker is staying in one area for too long. In the late 80s and early 90s, a lot of guys we know put all their money into primitive-style furniture and accessories—solid, utilitarian furniture and accessories with simple lines that have a distinctly "prairie" or "country" style. Back then, the primitive look was right-on. At that time, people were tired of looking at traditional mahogany and walnut furniture in their living rooms; they liked the simplicity and fun paint jobs and rough texture of this new style, which, actually, dates back to the 1860s.

Most primitives are made out of wood (oak and pine are popular materials) and come in strong shapes. Picture blocky benches and tables and large cabinet units given paint jobs in memorable colors like robin's-egg blue, yellow, and oxblood red, which have chipped and faded to look like they've been left out in the rain and sun too long.

For a good fifteen or twenty years, primitives were where the money was for pickers. People put everything they had into buying it: some dealers went to Asia and purchased reproduction primitives that were being made from antique wood—a construction method that allows new things to look a lot older than they actually are. (This is why at flea markets you see booths full of primitive accessories with a vaguely Eastern flair to them.)

Then, about five years ago, that ship sailed. In the mid-00s, the market for "country style" tanked and the taste of the masses evolved. Today people are looking for pieces with cleaner lines and a neater finish.

Sure, there's a chance that primitives will suddenly become the hot "new" thing in decorating again; revivals are par for the course in the world of design. But interior trends move a lot more slowly than they do in fashion, which changes every six months. It might take decades for primitives to have their resurgence. Personally, we don't know any picker who wants to wait that long, let alone anyone who can afford to.

Pickers have to be willing to adapt; they can't get pigeonholed into one area. These days, the public is demanding mid-century Modern furniture and a lot more Deco-inspired stuff. Dealers and buyers are following their lead. Any picker who expects to survive has to join them.

The only way that a picker can grow his business is to expand his knowledge base and develop his palette. That's how you evolve in business—and in life, too.

Mike and Frank in the shop.

ANTIQUE
ARCHAEOLOGY

A vintage car painted with the Antique Archaeology logo stands guard outside of the shop.

Frank and Mike check out a motorcycle in New Hampshire.

An old Volkswagen in Iowa — license plates are a popular collectible item.

NEVER MIND
THE DOG

BEWARE
OF
OWNER!

Even this warning doesn't scare the guys away!

Mike "picks" a new friend.

Mike's motorcycle at the Antique Archaeology shop.

AMERICAN
PICKERS

AMERICAN PICKERS

A WWII aviator cap picked by Mike in Georgia.

Going in for a closer look at a potential pick.

The guys with their trusty van.

Danielle puts her feet up at Antique Archaeology.

The Dream Team—Frank, Danielle, and Mike.

Mike and Frank "pop" on some treasures.

Frank takes a well-deserved break.

Goofing around at a pick.

Will it fit in the van? Then we'll take it!

AMERICAN
PICKER

Mike looking satisfied
after a successful pick.

Mike working the phone as he continues to pick.

AMERICAN PICKERS

Loading some vintage bikes into the van to take back to Antique Archaeology.

You never know what you're going to find.

7
BUYERS, BUYERS EVERYWHERE

HOW AND WHERE TO SELL YOUR PICKS

MORE EXPERIENCED PICKERS TAUGHT US TO ALWAYS HOLD BACK A FEW REALLY GOOD PICKS, BECAUSE YOU NEVER KNOW WHEN THINGS ARE GOING TO GET SLOW. IF YOUR MARKET DRIES UP ON YOU FOR SOME REASON, IT'S NICE TO HAVE A FEW PIECES IN THE BACK THAT YOU CAN SELL TO GET BY.

—Frank Fritz

Besides figuring out new ways to get old dirt stains out of blue jeans, the biggest challenge a picker faces is finding buyers for his finds.

Selling definitely isn't our favorite part of our job. Since we've stopped doing flea markets on a regular basis, making sales means spending a lot of time inside, on the phone and working on the Internet. And who wants to be doing that when you could be out picking?

But fact of the matter is that pickers are scrappers; we don't get a regular paycheck. If we don't buy and sell stuff, we're not making any money—and you can't pick on credit. We've got to have cash flow coming in at all times. And in order for that to happen, we've got to sell as much as we buy.

Some pickers we know live by the rule of "one in, two out." It's not a bad idea: you pop on one thing and to justify it you sell at least two things that you have sitting around. Keeps you on your toes. And, after all, things that are sitting around in a storage space are gathering dust, not interest. To make them pay, you've got to load 'em up and move 'em out.

THE DARK AGES OF PICKING

Twenty years ago, when we first started picking for a living, making out-of-town sales wasn't easy. Sure, you could set up at a flea market or get a booth in an antique mall and sell stuff all day long. But if you wanted to expand your business more than a few hundred miles, you had to be willing to spend a lot of time doing it. Once you figured out how to make it work and got into a good picking groove, you could make a ton of cash.

Mike was mainly dealing in bikes back in the day, finding them for cheap in barns and sheds around where we live in Iowa and selling them for big money to major collectors on the coasts. His memory of it:

Bikes were my main focus when I started picking seriously. All the pickers I knew told me they couldn't turn around without knocking one over, so I thought it'd be easy to hunt them down. But at first I had a much harder time finding the really valuable ones than I thought I would.

Back in the 90s, I knew guys in my area that were making a ton of money shipping bikes they found here to the coasts. It was crazy: less than twenty years ago, you could dig an old Schwinn from the 40s out from under a bunch of hay in a barn, give the guy $100 for it, and ship it to some guy in California who was ready to pay $1,000. I wanted in.

There were people running ads in trade journals and stuff—"Bicycle collectors looking for bikes"—those kinds of headlines. These guys were in New York and California and were looking for rare, really hard-to-find models. They didn't have that stuff where they live: we were in the Heartland, man! We were finding bikes inside every barn we saw. I got $3,000 for the first bike I sold—a Gormully & Jeffery Rambler that

GORMULLY & JEFFERY BICYCLES

R. Phillip Gormully and Thomas B. Jeffery built and sold bicycles from 1878 to 1900. This Chicago-based bicycle company's most famous contribution to the market is the Rambler, a bike that offered the most sophisticated engineering and detail when other companies were cutting corners. Introduced in the 1880s, it sold for about $100, a huge sum at the time. By 1900, Gormully and Jeffery was the second-largest bicycle-maker in the country. Jeffery sold his shares in the business in 1900 to pursue automobile invention and manufacturing.

someone threw in to the deal when I bought a Victor High-wheel from him for $1,500. So, I made $1,500 off the sale of the Rambler and got to keep the Highwheel.

Fifteen hundred dollars is a lot of money to a guy who is working for $5 an hour at a bicycle shop. When that's your situation and suddenly some guy gives you three Gs for something you basically got for free? You've just hit the mother lode. You're flying.

It was that sale that made me realize that the things I loved the most—old bicycles—were really valuable and that I could make a living selling them. And that's when I started calling myself a picker.

That was in the early 90s, back in the days before everyone was plugged into the Internet. (Cell phones weren't even around early in our careers—something that seems remarkable to us, looking back now.) When Mike was new to picking and didn't have a big list of regional buyers in his Rolodex that he could call on, in order to attract out-of-town customers he'd find them by placing classified ads and waiting for someone to give him a call.

If a buyer saw his ad and was interested in the bike Mike was selling, he'd call and ask for pictures—of course, he would want to see the bike he was buying before he popped. Understandable; we would, too. So, then Mike would take a few pictures of the bike from different angles with a Polaroid camera and send them to the maybe-buyer in the mail. Then he'd sit back and wait.

Sometimes it might take a week or two after the potential buyer got the snaps for him to call with a bid. Other times, he'd totally forget about it, and Mike would have to call him and check in—a long-distance call that back then could cost something like $12. It was a long, lengthy process, and a real pain.

In the long run, it was worth it if you managed to sell a bike to a big-time buyer with lots of friends. If you made that guy happy, then all his friends would start calling. And before you knew it, you had a network on your hands.

WHERE TO SELL

When we get back home from a big picking trip and start unloading the van, we immediately divide things into piles: "This goes to the flea market. That goes on the Internet. We should get Danielle to call Ken about that Mobile sign . . ."

Before Antique Archaeology opened, there were three main ways that we sold our picks: on the Internet, at flea markets, and by reach-

MOBIL FLYING PEGASUS LOGO

This mythical image was first used in 1911 by Standard Oil Company, which would spawn Mobilgas later that year. In the 1930s, the horse was given a "makeover": afterward, it flew left to right instead of right to left, which was its original orientation.

ing out to private clients. But that's really only scratching the surface of all the selling possibilities out there.

We've pulled together a few proven ways to sell that we've used ourselves over the years or that we know have worked well for other pickers. There's a strategy for every picking style.

The Flea Market

Flea markets are a great place for selling smalls and furniture that's not too hard to carry. Ideally, people want to be able to spend a little bit of money and come away with something really special, so we like to stock up on cool kitchen gear, unusual chalkware figures, dishes, paper memorabilia, toys, and other weird, cool collectibles that people have never seen before but—when they see it in your booth—suddenly decide they can't live without.

You've got to remember that people come to the flea market looking for deals. No one comes expecting to pay a lot of money: fleas are where many antique dealers come to stock their booths— they'll only pop on something if the price is where they can still sell it at a markup and, as Frank would say, it still needs to have meat on the bone. No one expects to pay antique-store prices: they want a bargain and they want to negotiate to get it. (Fleas are actually a great place to practice and test out bargaining skills that you can take on the road with you later.) That's fine: it's all part of the fun.

In the eastern part of the country, flea markets are like their own culture. They're everywhere in the South and up the East Coast—in

CHALKWARE

These sculpted gypsum figurines painted with watercolors had two major stints of popularity: first, in the late eighteenth century, and then again, after the Great Depression, when designs became kitschier.

small towns and big cities. We don't have that where we're from; flea markets just aren't as prevalent in Midwestern culture.

So, to get in on a little bit of that flea market love, the two of us used to drive once a month to sell at the one in Nashville—a town we both love to visit. It's full of antique dealers, interior designers, photographers, set decorators, and other professionals who like to buy the whackier stuff we sell to use in their work.

We like hitting the Nashville market, because there, as it is across the rest of the South, the flea market is a social event: the whole family goes and spends the day shopping. They split up in groups and hit their favorite dealers, who sometimes become their good friends.

Socializing can only do a picker so much good. You want to make sure that the flea where you choose to set up attracts lots of buyers—and not just any buyers: you want to hook up with a market where the buyers come looking for antiques and collectibles, not new stuff. If you're not really careful about choosing a quality market, you'll wind up trying to sell your killer pieces of old carnival memorabilia in a booth lodged between those being run by a sweet lady trying to market her homemade strawberry jam and a dude selling new acrylic gym socks out of plastic bins. Not a good match.

Of course, the South isn't the only place where flea market culture abounds. Almost every big city in the United States has one worth checking out—the Rose Bowl market in Pasadena, California, is one that always makes best-of lists, and there are good, solid regular markets in Chicago, Brooklyn, and Atlanta, too. These are the biggies; beginners probably want to skip setting up in that scene at first. Try looking for one of the smaller regional markets that seem to pop up in every community we pass through during the summer months.

And there's the weather—that's a big factor for flea market sellers. Some fleas are seasonal; they close down in the winter months. So, setting up there isn't a great choice if you're looking for a monthly gig. To be honest, pickers who sell at outside flea markets have to be pretty versatile. If it rains, you need a tarp. If it snows, you need a tarp and heating pads (not all booths have outlets to plug heaters into). And if it's 100 degrees in the shade and you don't have a pop-up tent? Well, then you just have to suffer.

One really nice thing about the flea market is that there is usually a flat set-up fee, depending on how big your booth space is and where it's located (inside usually costs more). After that, it's up to you to take care of the pricing and selling of your stuff. You load your own stuff in and out—and if you're from out of town, you save money on hotel rooms and sleep in your van. You'll be happy you did, early in the morning on the first day of the flea (they can last anywhere from a day to a full week), when dealers wake you up at four a.m. shining flashlights through the windows to see what's inside. That's actually when some of the best deals get made.

Antique Fairs

The only way antique fairs are different from flea markets is that they're a little bit more upscale. If you don't mind an *Archie* cartoon reference (who would?), antique fairs are like the Veronica to the flea market's Betty. Fairs are fancier, usually held in nicer places, and have more high-end collectibles than the flea, which is considered more down-market—even though the flea probably has some of the same things for sale as the fair and, more than likely, shares many of the same vendors.

It's all PR: the difference between the two is in the marketing. "Fair" sounds better than "flea"—that's just a fact. Rich people who would never set foot on a state fairground the weekend a flea market is in town get all their girlfriends together and have tea before they go drop a few grand at the "fair."

And you know what? That's awesome news for us. A picker doesn't care who buys the stuff in his booth as long as they're paying.

It might be harder to get permission to set up at a fair than a flea. There might be an application process, and you might be asked to leave certain items at home. Brand-name antiques, major pieces of architectural salvage, and small collectibles in perfect shape are what move here. Because they usually charge an entrance fee, there are going to be more serious buyers on hand, so you need to bring your A-game.

Fair setups are a lot like the flea: you pay one price for a certain space and take care of your own setup and sales. Just because it is a "fair," expect to pay a little more for the honor of being there. One bonus: the marketing budget is often better at antique fairs, which means more people with money to spend will find out you're there.

Yard Sales

Holding a yard sale—aka a garage sale, tag sale, or, if you're in a big city, stoop sale—is like having your own personal flea market, except setup is free and you can sell whatever the hell you want as long as it fits in your yard or in your carport. Like at the flea, you handle the money; just make sure you start out with a lot of change.

Advertising a yard sale is pretty easy. Five years ago, if you wanted anyone to show up at your sale, you had to buy an ad in the local newspaper classifieds to get the word out to the most people, but today, with all the online bulletin boards out there that offer free postings, this isn't really necessary. The days of pay-to-play in this arena are over. A lot of junkers plan their whole weekend shopping routes using their city's sale listings on Craigslist as a guide. They pop the addresses they find in the "For Sale" section into their GPS and just start driving. A tank of gas, a cup of strong coffee, and a pocket full of $1 bills is all any yard-sale lover really needs to be happy on an early Saturday morning.

When you're writing your own garage-sale listing, it's good to re-member that the more exciting words and details you add to your descriptions the higher the quality of buyers you're going to attract. Be specific and max out your word limit (most listing services have a word or character length you have to stay within). Instead of just say-ing, "I have a lot of old motorcycles," say, "This is a speed demon's dream sale! Hondas, Harleys, Indians, loose parts and wheels; pre-WWII Motorscoot. All in good condition." Now *that* is a sale worth waking up early for!

The only drawback of writing a good description is that the early birds are going to be chirping at your door hours before the advertised start time. If you don't want people bothering you before you've had your first cup of joe on the morning of the sale, or stopping by your house the day before, claiming that they have to work or have school the next day, asking if they can "pre-shop," flat-out say that in your ad. Not that anyone's going to pay attention: junkers are famous for making their own rules. But it doesn't hurt to say something anyway.

Antique Malls

In the days before eBay, if you wanted a more consistent cash flow than the flea market—it's hard to guarantee sales when you only have one weekend to make them—you'd have to rent a space in an antique mall.

When it comes to what you'll pay to sell there, the deal is usually the nicer the mall the higher the rent. But you've got to take into account that the extra money is going toward the upkeep, and probably helps attract shoppers with money, which is good if you have some expensive larger items that you don't want to bother selling at the flea—like big industrial pieces such as glass-front metal doctor's cabinets and old leather club-chairs, two decorator pieces that tend to move pretty quickly. Plus a lot of the higher-end joints even have Web sites and in-house auction sites that might charge lower fees than you'd pay posting on eBay.

Remember that rent isn't all you pay when you sell at a mall: most places charge 10 to 15 percent commission on every item you sell. You might also get charged for each credit card transaction that's made to sell your things. And payday is only once a month.

All that said, malls offer a pretty sweet deal to weekend pickers who don't have a lot of time to spend selling. All you have to do is stock your space and keep it looking good (a tip: the more time you can spend switching things up and adding new items to the mix the better your sales are going to be); the folks behind the counter take care of everything else for you.

Your Own Store

Give this one some very serious thought before you jump. A store may sound sexy and fun—easy even: find a place, move your stuff in, buy a cash register, and voilà! Instant income.

Not so fast, chief.

Who's going to manage the joint while you're out picking? Sure, you can open only a few days a week, but you're not doing yourself any favors when it comes to customer satisfaction. People like to shop at places that have reasonable hours; you can have the best store in the world with the most awesome picks for miles around. But if the hours are bad, you're not going to get the number of shoppers you need to stay open. Casually opening a store can be a self-defeating process. It only works if you put a lot of thought and effort into planning before-hand.

For example, weekends are great for picking—lots of yard sales and flea markets are only on Saturdays and Sundays—but they're also prime shopping days for nine-to-fivers who work during the week. If you're closed on the weekend, when they're out spending their paychecks, you're the one who loses.

Antique Archaeology was an online deal up until a few years ago; until business was really solid, it was almost impossible for us to keep a store up and keep picking as we needed to. Having a store costs a lot more than you think it would; not only do you have to pay rent and utilities, you have to hire someone like Danielle to manage the place and other people to work the sales floor. Then there's marketing and advertising costs, plus keeping up with taxes and credit card fees. And, to be a player in the retail world in the twenty-first century, your store has got to have a Web site, not to mention a Twitter and Facebook account that you keep up daily. (Believe us: if you work your business's social media, it *will* pay off in sales.)

On the plus side, having a store allows a picker to play decorator—you get to promote your own taste and identity inside the store with the displays. And since someone is there in the store all day, it's easier to share the history of the pieces with the buyer; you have a lot more control of the whole shopping experience than you do if your picks are sitting in an antique mall or even a booth at the flea market. The people who come into your store have chosen to be there, and you have the opportunity to make their visit memorable.

The Internet

Pickers have been around forever in some form or another. For thousands of years, the formula for what we do stayed pretty much the same: find, buy, sell, repeat—often, if possible.

But then eBay came along in the late 90s, and the entire industry got turned upside down. In ten short years, a system that had been passed down through families for dozens of generations did a complete 180.

The bottom line is that when the Internet revolution was good to a picker, it was very, very good. Selling online has made some pickers richer than they ever thought they could be selling junk. For the pickers who didn't adapt, it's been a career ender.

Fifteen years ago, the only way to sell the cool, weird, and really collectible treasures we found was by working our contacts. We had to know who was going to buy the 1930s bumper car or a jukebox before we popped or we knew we'd have to keep it until someone came into our network who wanted it. We still have to work the phones—Danielle is always following up with potential buyers when we snag something specific—but eBay means that we have a better chance of moving it if our other options fail.

The Internet gave us a worldwide market we'd have never been able to reach on our own; no matter how hard we worked. We didn't have to pick up the phone or write a letter to find buyers; they were online . . . along with every other seller in the picker universe. The competition definitely became more intense when eBay came along.

But it's not like eBay solves all of a picker's selling problems. You can't put just anything on there and boom! it sells. The things that are worth putting on eBay and other auction sites aren't the same things that are going to sell at the flea market; common things like dishes or tools aren't worth the fee you'd pay to post them online. To make money on the Internet, you have to offer things that are different and unusual. This is where you can sell the totally funky folk-art memory jug or regional gas-station signage from the 30s, and where you unload name-brand kitsch that you know has a big collector base, like hard-to-find *Star Wars* toys or *Scooby-Doo* lunch boxes. The online vintage-car market is totally booming; the same goes for bikes and anything else with wheels.

While the Internet has been great for educating people about really cool and unusual collectibles they never knew existed, it's also flooded the market with a lot of mediocre stuff. The problem with auction sites is that when a hundred people all try to sell the same *Dick Tracy* toy car, buyers go for the cheapest prices—or just don't pop on it, period: if the buyer is a hard-core collector, chances are they've already got this toy in their collection. Then the value of that piece drops across the board, proving that there really can be too much of a good thing.

On the up side, most Internet auction sites are easy to use; if you have a digital camera, a measuring tape, and can string a few sentences together to come up with a description, you're in business. But they're not free: you pay an insertion fee of anywhere from a quarter up to $4 for a plain listing (there are additional charges for posting something with a reserve price, which is the lowest price you'll accept). Then you have to pay eBay up to 15 percent or more of the final selling price. That adds up, which is why a lot of guys are moving on to other online options, including . . .

Craigslist

We've never really done a lot of selling on it, but the community-centric classified site Craigslist is how some pickers we know do all their business.

First of all, it's completely free. There are no charges to post and no fees to pay when you sell. The only drawback seems to be that the scope of your market is limited to one community at a time: you can only post one thing in one category every forty-eight hours in each city. The posting does stay up for a long time, though: up to forty-five days, compared to the maximum of ten on eBay (Craigslist postings expire in seven days in big cities like Boston, New York, and Chicago, so there you have to work fast). Also, you can only work one item in one city at a time, so if you're posting a vintage trombone for sale in Portland, Oregon, don't try putting the same ad on the Seattle, Washington, page of Craigslist: unless you wait until the first ad expires (or you choose to take it down), the powers-that-be will cite you for spamming.

As far as payment goes, you have total control. It's up to you whether or not to take credit cards or personal checks or if you just want to do everything via PayPal (a really quick, easy way to make a transaction: all you need is an e-mail address and a credit card and you're ready to rock). Heck, you can ask the buyer to pay you for the Volkswagen Beetle you're selling in nickels and pennies, if you want. It's up to you to determine those parameters, just make sure to specify it in the listing.

Other than selling things directly on Craigslist, a lot of pickers use it to plan their trips. Heading through Kansas? Check out the Wichita page to see what might be posted in the "collectibles" section, or click on "garage sales" and see what's going on the days you're there. It's a no-brainer, and probably the future of the online market.

EMOTIONAL ATTACHMENT = KISS OF DEATH

The biggest piece of advice we give to people who ask about starting a collection is to buy what you think is cool. To be good at your job as a picker, you have to be really into what you're buying; you have to have a real passion for it. As Mike likes to say, a true picker loves his or her stuff to the marrow.

Antique Archaeology is full of Mike's collections, which we use for decoration and inspiration—when the road has been hard on us, it's nice to come back to the store and be reminded of why we're doing this. People are always asking to buy the things they see there. The answer is usually no. People forget that we're collectors, too. The thrill we get out of finding things to add to our personal stashes is what keeps us driving when the going gets tough.

Having said that, pickers have to constantly remind themselves not to get too emotionally attached to things. We fall in deep, dark, mystical love with bikes we find on picks all the time, and it can be really hard to let them go, but you've got to be willing to cut the cord. Otherwise you're never going to make it in this business.

There are very, very few things either of us owns that we're not willing to get rid of if the right buyer offering the right amount of bank comes along at the exact right time.

To us, making money is always in the back of our minds. Down deep, it's always been all about the dollar. It may be hard to let something go, but once you sell, you've got an extra four grand on you, and, well, what are you going to do with that? If you're really sold on this way of life, you use it to fund your next trip.

GUESS YOU COULD call what we feel toward our collections "unsentimental attachment." We try to think of it in practical terms. For guys who deal in buying and selling memories, we're pretty cut-and-dry when it comes to getting rid of stuff.

Frank can tell it like it is:

There is nothing that I have that I wouldn't sell. Not a thing. I don't have anything that I can't find a replacement for somewhere. And I don't ever think that I've found the coolest thing in the world: I know that there might be something else out there that interests me more than what I've got.

I bought my first motorcycle—it's a Harley—when I was fifteen, and I still have that same bike. And I'd sell it tomorrow. I don't ride it anymore and I haven't started it in two or three years. I've had it for thirty-two years and it's time for someone else to ride it. As long as the offer is good, I'm happy to move it on out.

Never one of those people who love something so much that if someone threw a bunch of money at me I won't sell. It'd be gone. Because chances are if the guy is offering me stupid money for an antique hand-painted Guntherman toy or something, it'll be stupid enough to let me go and find two more to buy.

The key to splitting with a piece of your favorite collection is to wait until the right buyer comes along. It takes some experience to figure it out, but your gut will usually tell you when to let go. That's another reason a picker has to keep up with what's selling on the collectibles market.

GUNTHERMANN TOYS

The first toys produced by the Nuremberg, Germany, company were toy cars in 1898. Toys from the period of 1890 to 1919 can be identified by the logo of a circle with a shield inside, with the initials A.S.G.W.

A picker needs to know whether what he has in his collection is a solid future investment or something that he needs to go ahead and sell. If the market for a particular item is really high at the moment, and you're feeling less rich than you'd like to, it's probably a good idea to take the money. The only way you know what route to go is through experience and doing your homework.

For us, it usually all comes down to the buyer. If we meet someone who we can tell really appreciates the thing—someone who we can see respects how rare it is and acknowledges how valuable the item might be—they have a much better chance of taking it home than some picker with a fat wallet and tons of attitude. This is almost the reverse of what happens to us on picks, when the sellers are sizing us up, trying to figure out if we're fit owners of their treasures. Now it's our turn to choose.

Whatever happens, try not to lose sleep worrying about whether you made the right decision. When it comes right down to it, stuff is stuff. You can't take it with you.

8

THE PROFESSIONALS

MEET THE PEOPLE WHO NEED PICKERS

AS A PICKER, YOU CAN DRIVE YOURSELF CRAZY LOOKING FOR THE NEXT BIG THING IN THE ANTIQUES WORLD OR YOU CAN TALK TO A DECORATOR OR DESIGNER AND THEY CAN TELL YOU RIGHT NOW. THEY'RE THE TRENDSETTERS IN OUR WORLD.

—Mike Wolfe

W e're known for buying unusual things—no, scratch that. We're known for buying *weird* and unusual things.

And because these aren't the kinds of things that are embraced by the mainstream—not everyone needs a seven-foot-tall plastic boot or a pair of wearable Laurel & Hardy character heads—it's really important for us to have relationships with art and design professionals who like to work outside the box. Otherwise, some of our crazier picks would never move out of storage.

Over the years, we've accumulated a big client list of photographers, art directors, wardrobe stylists, set dressers, and graphic designers who call us up when they're looking for the perfectly rusted old gas-station sign, a Victorian top hat, or an antique barber's chair for some cool project they're working on.

We also get calls from storeowners from all over the country, who want to add a bit of our funky aesthetic to their shop. If you remember from the series, this is how we placed the large neon Masonic image we found at Judy's place in Ohio inside the Chicago men's store Isle of Man, and how a taxidermy boar's head we found somewhere in Michigan ended up staring down from the wall above the cash register at the denim company imogene+willie's store in Nashville.

Sometimes we reach out to these people ourselves; we end up introducing ourselves to the owners or managers of stores that have interiors we dig. Other times, our reputation precedes us, and clients recommend us to their creative friends. You never know who will end up hooking you up in that world.

Connections are how you grow in this business. A good example of that is how we met our friend Ruby, an art director in Tennessee.

RUBY, THE ART DIRECTOR

The only way to describe Ruby is to say that she's a total trip. She's funny and smart and talented as all get-out, and is the go-to art director and prop master in the South for photographers and directors who want cool and unique-looking sets for their projects. She's had a hand in the look of dozens of big movies (*Country Strong* and *Water for Elephants* are two) and has styled videos for everyone from Dolly Parton to The White Stripes to Taylor Swift.

We work with prop stylists like Ruby all the time. We love them because they're always looking for whacky things to put in their work.

I met Mike before I met Frank. It was four or five years ago, and we were introduced through a photographer in Nashville that he works with. (Funny story: the photographer got to know the guys when she bought something from them at the flea market here and they ended up keeping in touch, which led to sharing contacts. That's how things work in our world.)

Before we even met, Mike found out that I like old signs. He had figured out my e-mail and had been sending me pictures. One was of this old funky light-up hotel sign with arrows and lights on it—and I love anything with arrows and lights. I was hooked. I bought it sight-unseen, based on his word. He brought it to me here in Watertown and saw my warehouse and got an even better idea of the kind of things I do. After that, he started texting me pictures all the time.

When I'm buying from pickers as an art director or prop stylist, I'm not buying to resell, so I'm not going to haggle with them a lot. If they have something I need for my job, I value the price they have on it for its usefulness to me. I just ask what their best price is; I don't hear them say $40 and ask for $30. I don't care what it's worth on the market. I care about what it's worth to me to do my job well and fit within my budget.

I've learned to call Mike and Frank when I'm looking for obscure things. They're not the only pickers I use; you can't depend on two guys to get you everything you need. I don't waste time calling them if I'm looking for some mundane piece of furniture. That's not their deal.

Pickers like Mike and Frank are good for super-interesting, hard-to-find items. In fact, I just called Mike to tell him to keep his eyes open for an antique Victrola with a wooden horn. A big-time director I work with, who is based in London, wants me to find him one, and he's been very specific about what he wants. So, if I'm looking for something like that, I'll give the boys a call, because you never know what they might have seen in someone's garage the week before.

Set decorators have to create a lot of different worlds in their work; every set I work on can't resemble somewhere in Middle Tennessee, or Los Angeles, or Minneapolis, for that matter. My job is to convince the people watching the video or movie that they're somewhere else—in a different city or state, in a different decade, or even on a different planet. So I have to have a really broad range of resources available to me at all times.

For example, I just worked with a set designer on the movie Water for Elephants. This man has pickers all over the country; he has one woman in Florida whom he only calls for European draperies and curtains and linens. He has a different picker for practically every type of item he needs. But we're talking about serious professionals here: this guy's art department has *millions of dollars to spend. Usually what we do locally is small potatoes. They're still really interesting and cool jobs, but we don't always have huge budgets. So, I have to be more creative about how I find things.*

Personally, I'm a huge believer in picking serendipity. My theory is that in order for it to work, I have to put my needs out and spread them around like rice at a wedding. When I was working on that same movie, the production designer asked me to find real linoleum floor tiles. Now, these are really hard to find, but I was determined to do it. So, out of the blue, I called up a picker named Don in St. Louis, whom I very rarely call for stuff.

Don goes around stripping out old houses, so I thought I'd give it a shot. I called him and—unbelievable: the day before, he worked in a house covered in old linoleum. He got his son to take a picture of them for me, and when I saw it, I was really excited. It was patterned linoleum that was just perfect. I drove up to St. Louis to pick them up myself because I was so excited. And the designer was thrilled. We ended up making a runner, a kitchen counter, and another rug out of it.

This just goes to show you that you never know where the things you need are going to come from. From my experience, it's usually the last person—or picker—you'd ever expect.

Restaurant chains are another type of client pickers deal with. Big companies like Cracker Barrel and Ruby Tuesday hire buyers to go all over the country looking for nostalgic stuff to put in their restaurants. And when you start to think about how many Cracker Barrels you pass on a one hundred-mile stretch of road in the South, you understand why there's more than one guy out there picking for them.

The walls of those places are filled with old pictures and advertising signs; they hang old pots and pans and rusty farm tools from the freaking ceiling. Basically, they want to find things that have a bit of nostalgia to them—things that make a couple who stop by for fried catfish after church on Sunday point at an old Arm & Hammer sign on the wall and say, "Oh, remember when their baking soda boxes looked like that? I remember seeing that in my mom's kitchen . . ."

Remember the guy named Steve that we picked on the series who had, like, eight buildings full of stuff that he'd found for restaurants? That's the kind of volume those guys need. And they can't accumulate it all themselves; they need help, which is great news to pickers, because we're happy to unload some old signage or vintage fishing equipment or old taxidermy or whatever on them for a nice price. They usually have awesome budgets, which is always music to our ears.

WE GET CALLS every day from interior decorators asking us to find them something special. Or they're just checking in to find out what kind of stuff we've been turning up on the job. They're like us, in that they never want to let an interesting pick get past them. They'll say to us, "What'd you guys dig up? What are you finding for me?"

Designers and pickers really feed off each other's energy. Eight years ago, when Mike first walked into Serenite Maison, our friend Alex's store in Leiper's Fork, Tennessee, it was the first time he had ever been exposed to the French country look that is her signature. He asked her to show him around, and she took the time to explain why she liked the things she did—and we're talking things like Shabby Chic furniture; painted cast-iron lawn figures with paint chipping off them; cool sconces and other unusual light fixtures.

Once he figured out what made Alex tick, he started seeing the kind of purposefully worn but still really ornate stuff she loves almost everywhere we went. It's a weird thing, like when you learn a new word and suddenly you hear and read it everywhere. If you are exposed to a new look, for some reason, after that you're going to start seeing examples of it everywhere.

The relationships we have with designers are really important to us, both personally and financially, and we take them very seriously. We try to spend time with them—in their stores, if they have them (and a lot of the designers we work with do)—and figure out what gets their juices flowing. That way, when we're out on a pick, we know what kind of pieces are going to be worth bothering them about (we burn up the text message superhighway sending pictures of things to designers for them to say yea or nay on the spot). We keep lists of what our designer clients are looking for—mental ones for us to take on the road, and physical ones that are handwritten in about a million different notebooks back at the shop that Danielle keeps up—and try to check in with them as often as we can.

We've said it a dozen times before and we'll say it again: picking is all about building relationships. You've got to stay in touch to make them stronger.

ALEX, THE DESIGNER/ STORE OWNER

Alex is a designer (she's worked with Ozzy Osbourne, Pamela Anderson, and Ashley Judd and has tricked out the interiors of too many superstars' touring coaches to mention). She also owns an interior store, *plus* she used to be a picker herself. She's a total triple-threat!

Alex came to the rescue on the series when we pulled up to William Shatner's house outside of Louisville only to find it totally empty. Instead of picking, he wanted us to decorate the place.

Like we've said, we follow interior trends; we have to do our job well. But while we can definitely find and buy the stuff, we can't necessarily put it together—at least not in the way that he and his wife wanted.

So we rang up Alex at Serenite Maison, the antiques and accessories store she owns. In no time, she was in her car, driving up to go to work, ordering up picks and combining them with the Shatners' existing things in a killer office where they plan to run their horse business.

This was a totally one-off thing: we don't normally work with designers that closely. Our relationship with them is usually based entirely on sales.

But because Alex designs, owns a store, and has picked for a living, she's in a unique position in that she understands both sides of the coin when it comes to how a picker collaborates with decorators and store owners. Because there is a difference.

We asked her to share a little of her background and explain how pros like her work with guys like us:

The way I got started as a picker was really organic. When I lived in San Francisco, I loved going to flea markets and estate sales on the weekends. And, as it is in this business, when you're shopping in one area of the country most of the time, you start to see the same people lining up outside every sale. You get to know what they buy and what they do just by running into them so often. Sometimes you even get to be friends; I have a lot of great friends I met this way. Just going to an antique show is like old home week for me.

So, anyway, people would see me buying things that I liked—maybe I'd beat them to the punch on finding something cool, which always gets people's attention—and eventually they started stopping me and saying, "We see you all the time and we love what you pick. Would you consider being a picker for my store?" That's how I started doing it professionally. I picked for stores in San Francisco and for a store called Bountiful in L.A. for a long time before we moved to Tennessee.

Once I became a store owner, my wings were clipped a

little. I couldn't run around every day picking like I used to. I still go on picking trips a few times a year; I'm never going to give that up.

But the bottom line is, I need pickers because they're able to be out in the field when I can't. I can't fly off to Europe on long shopping trips like I used to, because of the store. But I can fly a few hours to meet a picker who has just had a container of new finds shipped in from England, and then arrange for those things to be shipped to me. And I can take the time to talk about picks over the phone or e-mail, and to have them bring stuff for me to see at the store.

All this background is to say, I get picking. I understand what the boys do; I know how much fun it is to be out there getting your hands dirty, but I also know how hard it is to find great stuff.

Picking is not easy. Designers give pickers big ol' lists of the things they want, but we know that the chance of them walking into the first place they see when they're out free-styling and finding that exact object in great condition with the perfect patina is really rare. Whenever that happens, it's like the angels have smiled upon you. To find great stuff, you usually have to kiss a lot of frogs, so to speak; you have to go through a lot of junk before you find a great score.

A lot of people think pickers can just go into a barn and find something amazing right off the bat. But besides the fact that cool items are becoming more and more rare, there are a lot of other things that can keep you from doing your job well. You have to be sharp to be a good picker. You have to have your wits about you all the time or you'll miss something important. If you're hungry or distracted or mad at the world, you might not be aware enough to notice the glue left over from a bad repair job that's still on the leg of the big farm table you're thinking about buying.

If you make bad decisions and start picking things that are no good, you're going to lose clients: I mean, I'm not going to buy that table, and I don't know a lot of designers and store owners buying for resale who would. So, you'd better be ready to be buried with it—you'd better dig a big fat jack grave, because that farm table is going into it with you.

Great pickers learn to be the eyes of their client. They understand that they're not spending their own money— unless, of course, they buy something that no one's going to want to buy.

I ask for a lot of information and I expect to get straight answers. When one of my pickers finds something they think I'll want, they take some pictures and text or e-mail them to me—our jobs are so much easier since everything went digital! They give me measurements and tell me about flaws or any-thing that might need to be repaired. All that information is really important—and it has to be correct. If I get a call and it's one of my guys saying, "Hey, I found a farm table like the one you wanted," then great! But if I buy it and pay to have it shipped here and I see that the leg isn't in good shape? Then you're in trouble: your days of picking for me are numbered.

Mike and Frank don't really do "chick picks." But that's the reason designers usually work with more than one picker. Each picker you work with might specialize in different things, like they might just work in lighting or only deal in statuary. I have a woman who picks for me who only brings me smalls—like the perfect little stack of linen napkins or the perfect set of old dishes. (All that little stuff takes a long time to find in good condition and she's great with the details.) So, a lot of times you might have a dozen pickers but they don't cross-pollinate; everyone has their own niche.

You have maybe a half-dozen strong ones that are your main sources; these are the ones who know your taste so well that they might as well be you out there picking. And when they're out looking and call you with something you might like, they nail it most of the time. Of course, they'll make mistakes, which is understandable; nobody can be on 100 percent of the time.

Something else about good pickers: they understand that people like me have to make a living. They get that I have to be able to turn a profit on the things they bring me. Since I have a retail store, I need to buy what they're selling at a price that's low enough to where I can get a little markup on it when I put it on the floor. A picker who's on it is thinking about this from the start: from the moment they pull the big metal urn out of the dirt in some guy's backyard, they know that the price they negotiate for it needs to be low enough to where they can up-sell it to me to up-sell again for my purposes.

This is another really important thing: you have to understand the antiques market to pick for people like me. Because if you don't know what the going price is for old sterling silver flatware, you won't be able to do the math to figure out where the markup has to be in order for me to buy it. And I'm not going to buy it if I know I can't roll it.

Sometimes this is a really quick process; sometimes it takes years. For instance, when I was working on the Shatners' house, I told Mike and Frank to be on the lookout for hat stands; they found several over the course of about a week. That's a really specific request, and when that project was over, I called off the hunt. But there are other things that my pickers know I'll always be looking for. I sell vintage tablecloths and napkins with monograms on them, and all the pickers I work with who deal in that kind of stuff know to call me when they find it.

Once a picker really, really gets what you like, it's amazing, because then they start bringing things to the table that I don't expect or never thought I'd want. They'll be, like, "Hey, I came across this brass case that looks like you. I know it's not a hat stand, which is what I usually bring you, but I thought you might like it. Is that something you're interested in?"

It's a two-way street. Sometimes one of my pickers will bring me something really, really cool and suggest a way to use it that I'd never thought of before. But then, on the same visit, I say to them, "Go out and find me a cool old dresser, because I'm going to drop a sink in it." And they go, "Really?!" I think we're kind of learning from each other.

There's always a lot of back-and-forth and a lot of dialogue. And there is a lot of excitement when someone nails it for you. Plus it's nice to know there's someone out working in the field for you that keeps you in mind and is interested in helping you grow your aesthetic. The idea that a picker might pop by tomorrow unexpectedly and show me something amazing that might take my eye in a totally new direction is just thrilling.

Like a lot of our clients, our relationship with Alex has moved past the work zone and become as much about friendship as business. When we're in her neck of the woods, we grab dinner. We now know her husband well; heck, we even know her dogs. We honestly enjoy her company, and we're pretty sure the feeling is mutual.

Becoming friends with the professionals we sell to isn't absolutely necessary to doing our thing. But we know it helps us get a better handle on their personalities and their likes and dislikes, which, in the end, helps us do a better job picking for them.

9
MANTIQUES

WHERE THE GUYS' THINGS ARE

PEOPLE THINK OF THE ANTIQUES WORLD AS A WHITE-COLLAR DOMAIN. MANTIQUES ARE MORE BLUE-COLLAR: THEY'RE ANTIQUES THAT ARE A LITTLE ROUGHER AROUND THE EDGES AND THAT APPEAL TO REGULAR GUYS—LIKE CARS, BIKES, SPORTS, GAMES, AND BEER-RELATED COLLECTIBLES. THEY'RE NOSTALGIC AND REMIND US OF FUN TIMES WE'VE HAD AND WHAT IT WAS LIKE TO BE A KID.

—Mike Wolfe

We're guys' guys—that's no big surprise to anyone who watches *American Pickers* and has seen how excited we get when we come across a rad 1920s bike frame or a weird old gadget. Sure, we can appreciate feminine things like linens and glassware and all that Shabby Chic stuff—the things that our designer friend Alex calls "chick picks." That doesn't mean we want to spend a lot of time looking at them, though.

Neither of us wants to drive 386 miles through the blowing snow, uphill all the way, just to stand in front of a locked case of carnival glass. If we're going to go through all that trouble, we want to get down and dirty and see some tough-looking stuff. Bring on the mantiques!

Mantiques have been around ever since the wheel was invented—which is kind of fitting, since wheeled things like old bikes, motorcycles, cars, scooters, and even skateboards are a big part of the whole scene. But it's not just rides that fall into the category of man-antiques: pieces of advertising, including neon and porcelain signs; memorabilia related to sports, automotive, tobacco, beer, rock and roll, and political parties; hunting, fishing, and outdoors or cabin-related items; kitsch collectibles like lava lamps, vintage issues of *Playboy*, pool tables, jukeboxes with cartoon characters and pop culture icons on the front (hello, Fonzie!), and toys all qualify as mantiques.

Put pretty simply, mantiques are any vintage item that makes a fifty-year-old guy remember what it's like to be a kid without any obligations and total freedom to run around having fun—whether his memories of times like that are of him at age five or twenty-five, mantiques help him create a space where he can flash back to a time when he had fewer responsibilities. Men we know with high-stress jobs (and even those with low-stress ones) and other major obligations sometimes create a "man cave" in their homes, somewhere that they can display their mantiques all in one place.

A man cave can be an area as small as a corner of a room or as large as an entire addition to their home; we know a lot of guys who get so excited about their manly collections that they sacrifice their garages to them; garages become shrines to their acquisitions. That's fine—whatever floats their boat. The bottom line is that they have a place to sit back, have a beer with their buddies, and relax in the presence of things that bring them happy memories and help them chill the heck out.

Another area of the mantiques market is the industrial design scene, which is probably one of the hottest looks going right now in that area. It's based on that rough and more-than-slightly-tumbled look that guys with less traditional taste in interiors tend to gravitate toward. A lot of the industrial furniture is repurposed or made from recycled materials, which gives it a casual, worn look that's very masculine.

YEAH, WE KNOW: mantiques is a pretty silly word. But it sounds better than saying "man antiques" all the time. Plus it's a term that's handy to be able to pull out of your back pocket, considering that the look has really caught on. There's even a high-end collectibles store in New York City now called Mantiques Modern, which is a big hit with interior designers hired to trick out man caves and bachelor pads with the kind of vintage leather sofas, hunting and fishing collectibles, old signs, and salvaged fixtures that we love so much. We're talking about antiques on steroids here.

Based on our own observations, here are the most mantique-y groupings of collectibles we deal with, along with some info on what to look for when you're scoping them out and ideas for how to use the stuff when you find it.

MOTORCYCLES, BIKES, AND CARS

It's no secret that guys like grease, and things that run on wheels have plenty of it.

When it comes to picking cycles, bikes, and cars, you're probably going to be buying them either to restore and ride or to salvage for parts. There is also a third option, which is buying for décor: in the right room, a nice empty shell of a vintage motorcycle does look pretty damn amazing. Either way, unless you have a ton of money to burn, you've got to tread carefully here.

Old rides with big brand names go for major coin, and if you're not absolutely sure what to look for, you're gonna get burned. As we've said before, knowing when to pop and when to pass only comes from experience and doing your homework. So, get studying.

Bicycles

The Midwest is where old bikes go to die. There are a lot of long-time bicycle enthusiasts there—not least of all Mike. He started dealing in antique bikes back in the mid-80s, when he could find amazing things in barns just a few miles away from home. He used to be able to find high-wheel bikes from the 1800s and balloon-tire bikes from the 1930s and get them for almost nothing—not many people knew what they were worth back then—and sell them to rich collectors on the West Coast for hundreds of dollars.

Thanks to eBay, today they do. There's still good stuff out there, but it's high-dollar picking. Older bikes are becoming harder and harder to find; one reason is that a lot of them were taken up during the scrap drives of WWII and melted down to make weapons and ammo. In addition to metals, scrap drives also rounded up lumber, rubber, paper, and other recyclable materials; donors were given a little cash payment and also got the satisfaction that they were helping the war effort.

Back then, this recycling boom was great for the military look-ing for raw materials and Americans looking for morale, but not so great for modern bike collectors, who now pay more for the honor. Really old bikes made before WWII in good condition can go for five figures, easy.

That's the high end. Casual collectors—and yes, most of them are men—can still find reasonably priced bikes for sale at flea mar-kets and yard sales. Chances are the older bikes you'll find will be girls' styles, which are the ones without the bar down the center between the handles and the seat. Why? Girls weren't jumping off curbs and taking their bikes apart so they could try and put them back together again. Girls took care of their bikes; boys didn't. So, there are a lot fewer boys'-style bikes around, which makes them more valuable in the end.

If you want to buy a secondhand bike to ride, you need to exam-ine it a bit more closely than you would if you were just buying it for display or to sell for parts. When you're giving it a once-over, make sure nothing is bent; the bike should be fairly symmetrical when it's balanced evenly on two tires. Check to see if the cables and chains are operational and not overly rusted. Look for cracks in tubing; bad tires can ruin a riding experience. If possible, have an expert examine it for you before you buy; have them give their opinion about what repairs might need to be done to make it operational again.

If you're going for authenticity, check to see if there are any signs that the bike has been repainted or that parts have been re-

BIKE BRANDS TO LOOK FOR

Bike names to look out for: Elgin; Victor/Victoria; Star; Columbia; Orient; Schwinn; Gormully & Jeffery.

placed (check to make sure that elements like pedals are identical on both sides). Ideally, everything will be original to the bike. Unfortunately, this is a rare occurrence in many old bikes: kids have always loved to customize and make their bikes their own by changing them up with accessories and extras. If you're looking for a 100 percent–authentic ride, you need to know as much about the brand and style of the bike you're inspecting—not to mention the era and even the year it was made. Knowing exactly what was specific to the original model is the key to making a direct match.

Again, the only way to know this is to expose yourself to as many bikes as you can—yes, that's more homework.

Cars

There are few things more beautiful to pickers like us than the sight of a wonderfully preserved antique car hiding under a drop cloth in someone's garage. Old cars are a hot commodity on the mantiques market, selling everywhere from a few hundred bucks for a beat-up Pinto from the 70s to over $40 million for big-time foreign collectibles like Bugattis and Rolls-Royces. (We might not need to point this out, but the majority of our picks have a lot more in common with the Pinto than the Rolls.)

Before you start poking around in a seller's garage, looking under drop cloths to see what you can see, you need to know your intentions for your new old car: do you want to find something that you can drive off the property, look for something you can drive after you have it tuned up or restored, or do you want to go the "rat rodder" route and find a ride you can chop up into pieces and reassemble or

CAR BRANDS TO LOOK FOR

A few car names to look out for: Studebaker; Plymouth; Ford Fairlane and Galaxie; Rolls-Royce; Nash; Chevelle; Cadillac Roadster.

sell for parts? And then there's always the option of doing what we did at Antique Archaeology when we painted our logo on a 1950 Nash instead of putting up a standard sign.

If you're buying for quality, a virgin paint job makes a car more desirable to most collectors, even if it's not in the best condition. Same goes for original parts: cars are always more valuable when they're sold with the same parts and finish that they rolled out of the factory with. The bottom line is that real collectors like to see what was there to begin with, not what the previous owner had the shop do to fix it up for sale.

Personally, we're rarely interested in cars that are already restored and look all polished and new. We're usually not buying them to fix them up; our hope is that we can buy it cheap, find a collector, and flip it fast—the last thing a working picker wants is to have a big old hunk of metal sitting in his garage, taking up valuable storage space.

Motorcycles and Scooters

Both of us have been riding motorcycles since we were teenagers, and we've been buying and flipping them—meaning selling them as quickly as we can—for almost as long. Just as we do with cars and bicycles, we buy motorcycles in different conditions, depending on what we want to do with them, how collectible they are, or how much we think we can get for them at resale.

When you're looking at an old motorcycle, the parts and the details are everything. The hubs, the frame, the transmission—all of these things matter. A dedicated collector—and that's the guy you

MOTORCYCLE BRANDS TO LOOK OUT FOR

A few motorcycle names to look out for: Harley-Davidson; Excelsior; Kawasaki; Flying Merkel; Indian; BSA; Honda; Knucklehead.

want to sell to, because he's going to pay the most—is going to be able to look at what you've got and tell everything but its fortune.

Again, the secret to collecting anything that rolls is to know what you're looking for. To accurately price a bike, you need to know how the models have changed through the years; the colors they did and didn't come in; the accessories they were sold with; and that's just the beginning. The more you know, the better deal you're going to get.

We're into old scooters, too—we like Vespas, especially really rare ones, like the Ape featured on the series that we found in Illinois. It's hard enough to find them in Europe, where they were made, but to turn one up in the Midwest was a total trip. Old trailers are cool, too—like the amazing 1934 Pre-Airstream we found in North Carolina, for example. Over the last few years, it's become trendy among a certain type of guy to buy an old trailer and retrofit it in a way that it's livable. We've heard of hipster kids in Southern California buying them on Craigslist, parking them in their backyards, and retrofitting the insides to turn them into mobile offices. Beats a regular office any day.

Gas Collectibles and Other Accessories

Car- and bike-related collectibles are a big deal in that collecting community. Even if they can't use them, collectors like to own items salvaged from service stations, like pumps and gas- and oil-related signs. Hard-core petroleum lovers dig *anything* to do with the car they love, so the same goes with old promotional shirts or hats, too.

Paper items like brochures and service manuals related to specific types of rare old cars are especially desirable when they're in good condition—like the DeLorean brochure that we found on the series in a garage in Ohio.

There were so few DeLoreans made—only nine thousand of the futuristic-looking sports cars rolled off the line during the two years they were produced, 1981 and 1982—and so few are estimated to still exist (only two-thirds of the total made are expected to still be in private hands or in circulation among collectors) that any little thing a picker can find that has to do with them is going to be valuable to a big car collector or even someone who has a thing for the ride in *Back to the Future*.

The brochure we picked up in Ohio wasn't something that came with the car; it was more or less a mini-publication that explained the model's features and its availability. But if we'd have come across the manual that came with the car and that was kept in the glove compartment (if DeLoreans even *have* glove compartments!), that'd have been better money than the $50 we were able to get for the material we popped on for $20.

But things like manuals rarely made it past the first owner, so if a collector can get his hands on a mint copy, he's in heaven.

SIGNAGE AND POSTERS

Old signs and posters are some of our favorite things to find; the graphics and colors are so much more interesting than what we have to choose from today. Because of this, a lot of guys would rather hang them on their walls than paintings or other "real" art.

The value of signs featuring advertising depends on the subject matter. Most guys want a sign with a subject that makes them seem tough, so we sell them a lot of gas, oil, and other service station–

related signs. Even if he can't change his oil, he can still look tough by hanging an old Gulf Oil sign in his study.

Gas stations used to have really amazing advertising. Fifty years ago, that was a big part of how they sold their brand. Companies in that era were just more thoughtful about design. Whether it was furniture or cars or graphic design, things seemed to be more pleasing to the eye.

Logos gas companies produced back then were more colorful—and, dare we say, a lot more fun. There were brighter graphics, bolder fonts, and a lot more animals used as mascots (again, a big attraction for sign collectors). Of all the animal motifs out there, Frank is most partial to Poly Oil, a company that used its title as play on words and advertised using a picture of a parrot.

Today, none of the big petrol companies seem to want to go back to the days of tigers (Exxon) and dinosaurs (Sinclair—though their brontosaurus still shows up on some signage). People just want to go to the station with the lowest price per gallon. If we had our way, people would gas up at the station with the coolest porcelain signs or the brightest neon lettering.

Pickers come across rusted or busted-up signs all the time; in most cases, they're not all that valuable. If you're buying for value, look for signs in good condition; if you're seeking them out for funky décor, you can be less choosy—good thing, since the really pristine signs are getting harder to find every day. Old neon signs in original working order are rare; all that exposed glass is hard to preserve. Enamel and porcelain signs usually fair a little better, but they're still fragile and tend to chip if they're not stored properly. Metal ones collect dings and holes: back when every kid had a BB gun, they were used as target practice. So, when a picker comes across a sign with cool subject matter, he jumps on it.

Another thing we're quick to buy is stand-alone letters. Shopkeepers would order different letters to spell out the store's name and then line them up on walls or attach them to the roof where passersby could see the finished name. We can't keep these things in stock: everyone loves them. People think it's cool to have one or both of their initials hanging over the stove in their kitchen or perched on top of the fridge.

Movie posters are a great substitute for paintings. You can find repop everywhere, but the real thing is harder to find—and a lot more expensive. A classic poster from a movie like *Star Wars* can go for hundreds of dollars, while those for newer movies cost a few bucks.

As you might guess, classics are popular because they allow people to feel nostalgic for the time period in which the movie was released—or maybe they're just hot for Princess Leia or something: for some collectors, a nice image of the opposite sex is a reason enough to buy.

When choosing posters to collect, graphic design freaks get into interesting fonts, like the "melting" letters that you find on monster films from the 50s and all the graphic "mod" lettering and bold color schemes that were popular in the late 60s and early 70s.

Men, in particular, tend to gravitate to specific genres, especially early horror films. Experts we talk to say posters from the Universal Horror era—think *Dracula, Frankenstein, Phantom of the Opera*, and all their ugly friends—move pretty fast on the collecting market, because, again, they strike a nostalgic chord. Plus, the animation is really striking. Also, we can't help thinking they probably appeal to guys who like modern horror films but aren't so crazy about the lame-o graphics on, say, a *Saw VI* movie poster. They don't make them like they used to—which is to say, fun, cartoonish, and a little campy; today, instead of a giant Creature from the Black Lagoon, all you get is a bloody hook lying on a cement floor: old scary beats new scary every time when it comes to graphics.

Until the mid-80s, an organization called the National Screen Ser-

COLLECTIBLE SIGNS AND MASCOTS TO LOOK OUT FOR

A few collectible signs and mascots to look out for: Mobilgas's Pegasus; Shell's yellow shell; Pontiac's red American Indian; Sinclair's dinosaur; Texaco's red star; Exxon's tiger; Citizens 77's blue greyhound.

vice was responsible for supplying theaters with movie posters. When a movie's run was over, the film house was supposed to return the poster to NSS; many didn't make it back to them, and ended up on fans' walls or in the possession of collectors. Older movie posters that bring the most money are, no big surprise, the ones in the best condition. You don't want pinholes, rips, or tears; ideally, the poster you buy will have been stored flat or rolled, not folded. Traditional signs are 27×40 inches and are called "one sheets."

Other posters we've come across on picks were printed as part of the propaganda push during the two world wars, which were used to justify each side's position, as well as encouraging young guys to enlist in the military and reminding people to be thrifty ("Food Is Ammunition—Don't Waste It," for example). The graphics on these early posters are bold and colors are muted, which makes them look kind of elegant. Our friend Judy in Ohio is a big WWI poster collector. She let us know that reproductions abound in this area; you can tell them by the weight of the paper: original posters were thin, like newsprint, while newer reprints are thick.

THE INDUSTRIAL AND SALVAGE SCENES

Recycling has really taken off in the worlds of architecture and interior design. Twenty years ago, mainstream trends were totally different: people wanted their homes to be filled with sleek, new furniture and contemporary art. Of course, there have always been some people who have loved recycled style—the whole Shabby Chic craze that took off in America in the 80s is proof of that. Today, though, people are actually asking designers to make their houses look like the inside of a retro factory building (exposed brick, cement floors) or the interior of a weathered barn (exposed beams, chipped paint), using reclaimed building materials and secondhand furniture.

Guys who are taking the time to restore older homes or to retrofit vintage office buildings for modern uses are recognizing that it's cool to keep a joint's original elements in play. If they do have to buy something to fill in the blanks, they want it to be secondhand or made from salvaged materials, preferably American-made. Music to a mantiquer's ears: we see this stuff all the time.

These architectural remnants don't necessarily have to be big; great-looking hardware for doors and windows, sink and light fixtures, or heavy-duty grating salvaged from old homes or buildings are in demand at all times. Pickers who keep their eyes peeled can find this stuff all over the place.

On the series, we've come across some really memorable lighting, like the old hanging lamps that we found in South Carolina. Mary, the woman who sold them to Mike, said they came out of a church that her father helped build back in the early part of the last century; when the church was renovated years later, they got rid of them—and her father brought them home.

In some ways, they were part of her family history, but she had never been able to use them and was happy to sell them to us so that we could find a new home for them, like outside the door of someone's cool loft apartment in some old retrofitted factory or in the foyer of a gothic-style house with high ceilings, where heavy iron fixtures look right at home.

Industrial style is also hot right now, and guys in particular seem to like the brushed-metal lab tables, heavy-duty office chairs, and those big, cone-shaped metal pendant lamps—you know, the ones that were originally made to hang over worktables in factories but now show up in modern kitchens all the time. Another good example is how those low rolling carts with the big cast-iron wheels are being used as coffee tables. (All you have to do is give them a good power wash, throw a coat of wax on the wood, and they're ready to rock.)

We rescue these things from old factories or abandoned storage spaces from the middle part of the last century and sell them directly to interior stores or designers who know this kind of stuff looks awesome against an exposed brick wall.

Mike's a big fan of the industrial look. One of his favorite industrial pieces is the desk in his office at Antique Archaeology, which he salvaged from a factory in Rock Island, Illinois. The top is made of thick, worn wood; industrial pieces normally look like they've been used quite a bit—part of their charm and something that reminds the owner that they have a history all their own: someone made a living at this desk for thirty years before Mike got his hands on it, which is a cool thing to think about. The base and legs are heavy iron.

TOYS AND KITSCH

Anyone who thinks toys are for kids has obviously never been to either of our homes. You're never too old for this stuff.

Like a lot of guys, both of us like collecting old toys. It's another one of those nostalgia trips we take doing this job: we really like finding boxes full of the same kind of plastic GI Joe action dolls we played with as kids, or the same *Planet of the Apes* lunch box one of us carried to school in fifth grade. But that's only part of the reason we like them.

Old toys look cool. And while the ones we played with back in the late 60s and early 70s are fine and everything, plastic materials aren't what really gets our picker blood pumping. We love the lines and mechanisms of the early cast-iron and tin-plate toys. A lot of the really valuable ones were made overseas, in Germany and Japan, and were painted by hand.

If you find older toys in good condition—meaning all moving elements like wind-up keys, pull-strings, and battery-operated parts are in working order, and all its accessories are intact (a lot of toy cars are missing tires, for example)—they're worth a lot of dough. (If you find something in its original box, there's even more *dinero* waiting for you at resell.)

As for what to do with them: if you're not going to play with them (hey, don't knock it till you've tried it), then use them as decoration. We've been in some really swank bachelor pads that have tin toys lined up on the bookshelves in the study or out on a side table to use as a conversation-starter.

When we say kitsch, we're talking fun, weird things, from funkier pieces of early folk art like hand-carved wooden animals, crude paintings, and homemade pottery (amateur artists' mistakes sometimes look a lot more appealing to us than a perfect product!) all the way up to, say, early 80s skateboards and Pac-Man arcade machines. Some of the most interesting and man-centric kitsch we've come across on the series has been the out-there souvenirs that servicemen used to bring back from their stations in WWII through Vietnam. We've popped on hula girl lamps with swiveling hips that hailed from Hawaii, circa the early 40s, and portraits of exotic ladies painted on black velvet that came back from the Pacific Rim.

Kitsch is really plentiful; almost every yard sale and flea market out there has a few odd pieces of homemade art or a door wreath made out of layers of Budweiser pop-tops (yes, they exist). That makes it easy for anyone to start and build a collection pretty quickly.

It's usually pretty cheap, too—well, it can be. Kitsch collectibles like, say, a souvenir mug from Yellowstone National Park circa 1960 that was mass-produced and that is, therefore, easy to find may

TOY BRANDS TO LOOK OUT FOR

Some toy brands to look out for: Gunthermann; Steiff; Keystone; Gottschalk; Marklin; Wilkins; Schuco; Dinky.

only be worth a few bucks, while rare folk art by guys like Howard Finster and Henry Darger is worth thousands of dollars. As for the hula girl? You can probably get her for a good bit less.

MACHINES AND OTHER TOOLS

There's a huge male market out there for coin-operated machines and other gadget-y collectibles. Contraptions like vintage peanut dispensers or standup scales and old-fashioned grip testers—you know, the ones that used to be stationed in the front of grocery stores to keep kids shopping with their mothers happy—might all look pretty damn cool hanging out in a really masculine house. Imagine a neon jukebox filled with the same records it held back in the 50s spinning in someone's living room, or a pinball machine from the 70s or 80s tilting away beside a pool table in the den.

Speaking of pinball machines, we've picked a few in our day. The ones that are the most valuable have cool pop-culture subject matter as their theme. Frank picked a KISS machine not long ago, thinking that it would appeal to both music fans and major pinball collectors. That's another good thing about buying machines with popular themes like cartoons or TV shows: you automatically double your audience if you decide to sell.

Other mantiques we slide under the machine category are weird old tools, flashlights, cameras, and projectors. Back to the industrial design trend for a minute: within that movement, there's a real demand for decorative objects that look mechanical to balance out the rawness of, say, the exposed brick wall or raw concrete floor that you might find in some guy's industrial-style apartment. A boxy old-school camera with a big round flash looks really great mixed in with more streamlined items on a shelf.

HUNTING AND MILITARY

Vintage hunting and military collectibles—think artillery, uniforms, army/navy surplus, as well as fishing gear, taxidermy, and basically anything else that has to do with trapping animals—are another area of the mantique world that trades really heavy on nostalgia. A lot of times guys will buy this outdoorsy stuff because it reminds them of their fathers or grandfathers, and how maybe they fought overseas when they were younger or how they used to like to go dove-hunting in the fall. Dudes who are into the Americana scene also like finding and wearing old military-issue bomber jackets and enjoy having collections of interesting-looking medals and badges in their homes.

In the series, we've bought quite a few things related to the military, including a leather pilot's skull cap from WWII with some headset gear still inside. On the hunting end of things, we picked a way-cool Bausch & Lomb spotting telescope issued by the NRA.

Taxidermy falls under this category, too. It used to be that only hunters or fishermen had stuffed animals hanging on their walls. Now preserved birds in flight; oversized elk and deer heads with big racks of antlers; and fat, shiny fish forever frozen in mid-jump are everywhere—looking down from the walls of upscale restaurants and boutiques to high-end living rooms in private homes. Think about how much fun it would be to come home to a giant black bear standing by the front door, welcoming you with its outstretched arms like some hairy zombie!

Deer, fish, and birds are everywhere (migratory birds like ducks and geese are actually illegal to buy or sell, so avoid those); we like to focus on the unusual taxidermy pieces. One of the weirdest we've ever come across was the stuffed miniature pony we bought from Lester, a collector we picked in Illinois. (We passed on his stuffed chimp, Skippy, because the monkey's face had deteriorated—a common problem with older taxidermy and pieces that have been exposed to too much heat; plus, that thing *stank* worse than swamp rot.) Rare pieces like our little horse—which, we found out, was probably used by a leather-maker to display children's saddles—are valued based on condition. Obviously, the better they've been preserved the more they're worth.

Even without ears, our pony still made us a $400 profit. We bought him for $200 but sold him to the appraiser from Lexington, Kentucky, that we contacted to find out how much he was worth, for a cool $600.

10
WHAT'S NEXT?
THE FUTURE OF PICKING

ONE THING ABOUT BEING ON THE ROAD ALL THE TIME IS THAT WE NEVER KNOW WHERE WE'RE GONNA END UP. WE CAN HAVE A CONVERSATION WITH SOMEBODY, AND WE GO THIS WAY, ANOTHER ONE, AND WE GO THAT WAY. THAT'S THE DIF-FERENCE BETWEEN NINE-TO-FIVERS AND US.

—Mike Wolfe

As pickers, we count on being surprised every day. We literally never know what we're going to find when we open a door to an old shed or pull down one of those drop-down staircases to climb up into someone's packed attic.

No day is ever the same in a picker's world. You can never walk into the same barn twice, you know? Even if you've been there before, the picking is always different. Change is the only constant in this gig.

Because we have to always roll with the punches, we're never thinking too far ahead, as far as our careers go. If you start spending too much time worrying about the future, you're going to get anxious and end up missing all the picks you could be getting to today.

What if no one wants to buy old metal signs from us anymore? (Not likely: the demand for quality vintage stuff is always going to be there.) What happens when all the old collectors with the coolest stuff pass away? (Twenty acres of amazing picks won't just vanish into the air. Chances are it's just waiting on a new owner.) What if all those old rusting motorcycles we love to pop on suddenly stop turning up? (Not going to happen in our lifetime—the types of things we pick are constantly evolving: what we're buying now is completely different from what we were buying ten years ago. Plus, newer bikes will eventually become antiques, so there's a pretty constant supply.)

Regarding the stock of future: for a long time, the collectors' rule of thumb was that anything made more than thirty years ago could be considered an antique. Up until twenty or so years ago, that number might have made some sense. But today, these prospective antiques are mass-produced in overseas factories. The quality and care that goes into them isn't the same as it once was; we live in a throwaway society. Take bicycles, for example.

As recently as two decades ago, most people were still buying their bikes from specialty stores; a salesman was there to help them find the perfect match, choosing from a variety of styles that were sturdy, built to last, and made in the States. Today, most folks go to big-box department stores to buy bikes that were produced and assembled in China.

The truth is that these bicycles are never going to be as collectible as the ones that were made by a relatively small team of U.S. workers who were paid to care about good design and construction, and were invested in creating quality products.

Across the board, from bikes to furniture to clothing, the items that are going to be the most collectible in thirty-plus years are things being handmade by specialized artisans. In terms of bikes, we're talking about the guys out there who spend days crafting handmade frames and parts in their little studios. They have total quality control over their creations, every single step of the way. If something goes awry in their design, they can fix it immediately. They believe in quality, not quantity. Now, *this* is the kind of a bike a future collector will want to have in his stash!

There are a few problems with this system. One, these bikes are expensive. There's a pretty specific audience that can justify spending several grand on a handmade bike to ride. Two, the process is time-consuming. Even with a modest demand, the artisan bike community can barely keep up. If the production numbers are already limited, just imagine how rare bikes like these, in good condition, are going to be in several decades, after they've been ridden and wrecked and generally loved as much as they were made to be for years on end.

Not every bike survives that kind of tough love in order to become a collectible, which means the pool of quality future picks is getting smaller. But that's not necessarily a bad thing. It just means that in our kids' world, collecting is going to be a much more time-intensive and focused hobby and, more than likely, a more expensive one than it's been for guys our age.

WE'VE SEEN THE picking industry go through massive changes in the past. As we've said before, thanks to Internet auctions, over the course of just a few years, people who never had even the slightest interest in antiques were waking up to the fact that Grandma's old camel-back trunk rotting away in the corner of their cellar might actually be worth something.

Of course, you know how that one's playing out, via a flooded collectibles market, inflated prices, and hundreds of antique malls and stores going out of business because they couldn't hold up against that massive competition. But eBay has also been a great way to learn about collectibles you've never heard of before and an awesome place to buy weird, whacky stuff from around the world that you'd have never dreamed were out there.

No doubt, eventually there will be "another eBay"—something else major to shake up the picking market and change the way we do business. Maybe it will be computer-related, maybe not. Who knows—maybe people will suddenly decide that they have to be able to touch and feel things themselves before they buy, which will lead us back to the old model of brick-and-mortar shopping across the board. Again, change is inevitable. It's just a matter of time. And when the new phase of picking happens, we'll just have to roll with the punches as they come.

Worrying about all that now is just going to take your eyes off the prize. You've got to live in the moment and stay focused on your next pick.

IT'S ALL ABOUT THE KIDS

As we've said many times before, in this book, we believe that picking is about a lot more than just making money; it's about history and making connections and community.

The stories we hear from the people we pick are priceless—and fragile, too. The only way to keep them alive is to teach the next generation to value this information and treat it with care. So, really, the most important thing pickers can do to make sure that their legacy is carried on is to pass what they know to their kids and grandkids.

We've taken several kids picking with us on our series—including Mike's nephew, Reese—and it's always been a total blast and really eye-opening. Kids totally dig picking; they think it's fun—which it is, of course.

And it's educational, too—something that more parents and teachers need to remember. If it were up to us, schools would take kids on field trips through junkyards so that they could see that things were once made in the States—that we were manufacturers, not just consumers. Trash can teach you a lot. And even though going picking can be a learning experience, it's not something that has to be sugarcoated to seem like a good time: there may be a history lesson on the inside, but to a kid, going picking looks like an adventure. What kid doesn't love a treasure hunt, which, again, is really what this whole business is all about?

We get letters and e-mails from kids all over the country who love to go on their own picks. They watch the series, take notes, and head out into their backyards to see what they can dig up under the trees or find on the side of the street in their neighborhoods. We have parents telling us that their kids are starting to think in a different way about the things they come across every day. They're realizing that everything they use—the chairs they sit on, the books they read, the cars that take them to school, whatever—has a past and a future.

Just because it's old doesn't mean it's no good—and that's Recycling 101, folks.

Finally—and this is maybe the coolest thing of all—we hear stories of kids bonding with their parents and grandparents in new ways, thanks to picking. *American Pickers* is teaching them that almost every family's history can be told through the items that have been passed down from generation to generation. We hear about kids who are suddenly taking an interest in their family's past, and seeking out older family members to show them the heirlooms that make up their own back-story and to share the stories that go along with them.

In the process, the kids pick up the message that the stuff they're finding is only part of the deal. The real thrill of picking is in the discovery of new ideas and in the connections they make with the people in their family and communities.

SOME INSPIRATION BEFORE WE GO

So, that's it—that's the *American Pickers'* take on junking for fun and profit.

To anyone thinking about taking on picking as a full-time job after reading this book, we say, good luck. We can't tell you that this is an easy life. But we can tell you that once you get going, it's a good one.

Pickers make their own schedules, they set their own hours, they're their own bosses—and all that's really nice. Because when picking is good, it's very, very good. But when it's bad . . . you know the rest.

Dry times hit every picker. They're never permanent, though. You just have to work through them. The key to making life as a picker work is to really love what you do, to value the things you pick, and respect the people you meet along the way.

When Mike was first starting out, he got some great advice from an old pro:

When I first started thinking about going into business for myself, I met an old picker from Wisconsin who had been doing it forever. We would see each other at the swap meets and stuff, and he would always stop by the table where I was set up to see what I was selling. He'd say, "You got a good eye. You know what you're doing. Have you ever thought about going full-time?"

I was, like, No way, man. There's no way I could give up my job at the bike shop and the security of that to do this. It's too dangerous. It's too scary. I don't know if I'd ever be able to find enough stuff.

He would continue to encourage me. "I think you can do it. I see the things you buy and what you sell it for. I see the way you are around people. I think you can make a living doing this."

And, of course, he was right. I always remember another thing he told me, too. When he first started out, he tried to buy and sell something every single day. He was hungry; he wanted to learn and to make it work.

I still think that's good advice—and not just for beginners. I never want to lose touch with what it feels like to be hungry. Because if I do, then I'll lose touch with why I really love what I do.

PICKER SPEAK

Breaking the ice: Buying something small from a reluctant picker in order to get him in the selling mood. One sale can lead to more.

Bruiser: Big, heavy pick.

A buck: $100. Also, a buck-fifty is $150.

Cash money: The price if you're paying in dollars, on the spot.

Cold call: Knocking on someone's door unannounced.

Crazy money: aka "stupid money." The high-end price a seller wants for an item. Sometimes we give them that so they feel in control.

Emotional affair: When you're picking with your heart, not your brain. Lusting over an item can sometimes lead to making bad business deals.

Farm fresh: Something that is newly picked. For dealers these are the most desirable items, since they're the first pros to see them.

Free-styling: Driving around looking for places to pick with no real destination in mind. Picking by the seat of your pants, if you will.

A "G": $1,000.

Honey hole: A stop that's chock-full of amazing stuff the owner is ready to sell. When you find one, get down and kiss Mother Earth to thank her for your good luck.

Meat on the bone: An item you purchase for a low enough price that you'll surely make a profit when you resell.

Mega-pick: A pick with tons of volume. Mega-picks get confused with honey holes a lot but they're totally different. A mega-pick is all about quantity; a honey hole has quantity, too, but it also has quality going for it.

NFS: The acronym for "not for sale."

NOS: New Old Stock. It might be old, but it's stock that's still in the box, as if it were tucked in a time machine in 1950 and sent to 2011, ready to sell today.

Pop on that: Sold! As in, "Three porcelain gas station signs for $20? I'll pop on that." Another way of saying it is "pull the trigger." It's also onomatopoeia: when you're excited you wanna pop!

Primary search: The initial visual scan a picker gives a new picking space, in which he notes large items and things that can be seen without opening doors or pulling out drawers.

Roached: Rusted, busted, or otherwise destroyed (sometimes this is a good thing).

Rusty gold: Awesome junk, a picker's delight.

Secondary search: It follows the primary search and involves digging through closets and drawers, looking behind furniture, under rugs, and inside glove compartments to see what is there.

Slow your roll: Code for taking your time and really thinking about what you're buying before you lay down any money.

Small: An antique that's physically smaller than, say, a piece of furniture. In antique malls, you'll find them in display cases. Smalls can be bigger than a breadbox, but rarely will a small be too heavy for one person to carry.

Step up to the plate: Meet them where they are; pay what the seller wants.

Style cramper: Anything that makes picking more difficult than it already is. For instance, a flat tire or a difficult relative trying to influence the seller.

Tonnage, buildup: Accumulations of fabulous, wonderful junk.

Triple-pick: A mega-pick that's got more than just one layer. Usually you don't need to visit a site more than three times; if you're any good at what you do, you'll get it all in three visits.

Windshield time: Time spent free-styling, just cruising around on back roads, looking for a honey hole to get caught in.

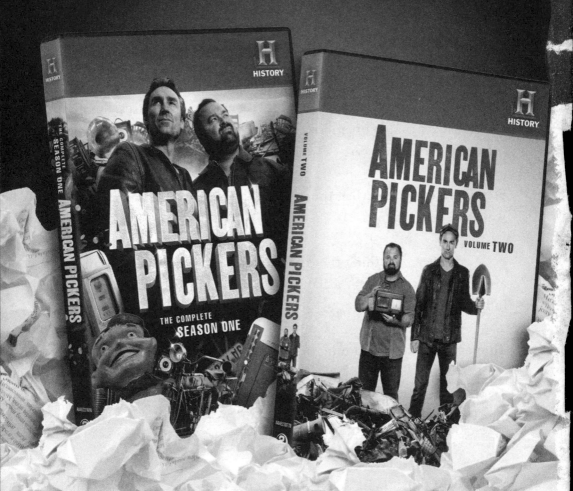

Here are a couple of DVDs
YOU DEFINITELY DON'T WANT TO THROW IN THE TRASH

AMERICAN PICKERS
now available wherever DVDs are sold